DROSTE

Düsseldorf

Discover the city

Overlooking Düsseldorf and the Rhine

DÜSSELDORF, MY LOVE

How do you get to this huge village on the Düssel? By car? By boat? By plane? By train? Düsseldorf has many faces and there are many ways to get there. You can even get there by underground, which was built in the 80s. You can't compare the underground with the one in New York or Tokyo, but there it is.

Speaking about size we should perhaps mention the name. Part of the name is "dorf" which means village and in a way this holds true. Düsseldorf is a big city with 600 000 inhabitants (still growing) but at the same time not that big, it has quiet areas, you feel at ease and many of its sights can be reached on foot, so "dorf" isn't that wrong, after all.

Well, the name: historians believe that the first settlements in the early middle ages were nearer to the Düssel than to the Rhine. It seems that people then preferred the small Düssel to the big river Rhine. The Düssel originates in Wuppertal and joins the Rhine close to the Altstadt.

In 1135 – first recorded mention of "Düsseldorp" – the name was decided on and never given up. In 1288, after the victory in the battle of Worringen, Count Adolf von Berg proclaimed Düsseldorf to be a town. It was after the battle that the Düsseldorfers stood up against a ruler from Cologne – this historical event is commemorated with an impressive painting in the Jan-Wellem-Room in the Rathaus (Town Hall).

Düsseldorf today

Those times have passed. Probably most of the Düsseldorfers haven't got a clue about the battle of Worringen. Why should they? They have other things on their minds. A Düsseldorfer is the incarnation of a Rhinelander: Easy-going, happy to talk to strangers, interested and curious. Lively and fond of partying he is happy to say: "Let's go where the music plays" He wouldn't miss a party; if only to gossip and above all to make jokes about it. That's what they really like, giving their opinions, knowing things better. But, in the end, they have to concede: "Live and let live".

This leads us directly to Königsallee, the place where you can give yourself a treat: a world-famous shopping mile, a sort of huge catwalk. It's a stage for those who like showing off and for professional models. Open all year, slightly changing daily performances, never ending repetitions; no matter what you see, it's never boring and much better than TV.

The Düsseldorfers or them visitor sits in the first row, in a café and enjoys the spectacle, pleased to sit there and watch the big show that's going on and of course he's part of it: Let's be where the music plays!

Top-class culture

Theatre? Let's talk about culture. Düsseldorf is well known for its high-standard of culture. Gustaf Gründgens was the director of the theatre from 1947 to 1955. Robert Schumann lived and worked there in the mid-19th century, Goethe often stayed with the Jacobi family in today's Malkasten. The Kunstakademie (Academy of Art) was founded by Elector Carl Theodor.

Königsallee with Kö-Graben

Heinrich Heine

The building still exists and many artists have come from there: Pankok, Mataré, Klee, Beuys and in recent times Andreas Gursky, Markus Lüpertz, Jörg Immendorff (who died in 2007). The Düsseldorf School of Painting stands for realistic paintings of landscapes and people, well known names are Clarenbach and Achenbach.

The most famous poet that Düsseldorf knows well how to use for marketing methods these days is Heinrich Heine. He was born in Bolkerstraße and went to school in the city center as well. He later went to Paris into exile and criticized Germany in quite a lot of his literary works. However, at some point of time Düsseldorf came to appreciate this great Jewish writer and nowadays commemorates him by naming important sights and institutions after him: Heinrich-Heine-Universität, Heinrich-Heine-Allee and Heine-Institut, to name just a few. A monument was set up in his honor on the border of Carlstadt and has caused many controversial conversations ever since.

World's longest bar counter and much more

Many tourists only relate Düsseldorf to Altbier and are practically searching for „World's longest bar counter". This term derives from the fact that there are more than 250 bars and restaurants clustered within an area of about 500 square meters rather than one continuous bar. Bolkerstraße and the surrounding streets are mainly frequented by people who enjoy heavy drinking and partying their heart out. Young people in costumes come to celebrate stag nights from all over Germany. There is a good mix of Irish pubs, cocktail bars, fast food restaurants and of course the famous breweries which brew their own
Altbier. Their names are Uerige, Füchschen, Schlüssel, Schumacher and Kürzer and most of them date back to the 19th century.

The Altstadt is small, lively and has many faces. There is St Lambertus, an old basilica with a turned and crooked tower. The Stiftsplatz in front of this church is like an oasis, quiet and peaceful like the central place in a small village. Not even a stone's throw away is Ratinger Straße with its legendary pubs **Uel** and **Ohme Jupp** – popular among Düsseldorfers. The bars on Bolker Straße are highly tourists.

Flinger Straße and Berger Straße are shopping streets as well

Old town

as Carlsplatz, a historical part of the Altstadt. There are nice shops such as small jewellers, antique shops and fashion shops.

Scattered all over the area are museums and cultural institutions: K20 and Kunsthalle at **Grabbeplatz, Heine-Haus** in Bolkerstraße, the **opera house** in Heinrich-Heine-Allee, the **Kom(m)ödchen** in the basement of the **Kunsthalle, Institut Français, Heinrich-Heine-Institut, Marionetten-Theater** (puppet show) on Bilker Straße and the **Stadtmuseum** (Spee'scher Graben).

They all form part of the Altstadt, every part a little piece of art on its own and worth visiting. Put them together you have an important and big lump of lovable Düsseldorf.

Thriving economy

Speaking of importance: it is the capital of the Bundesland with the highest population. In economic terms, it easily competes with Munich, Stuttgart, Hamburg or Frankfurt and fights them when investments are at stake. Düsseldorf is the only big city in Germany without debts; it's unbelievable considering the financial problems Cologne or Berlin have. It's not a question of saving money – Düsseldorfers are quite generous in spending money but they have a strong and successful economy.

With the turn of the millennium Düsseldorf started booming to a higher degree than its inhabitants realize. Big companies like E.on and Henkel have their headoffices or important branches there. International law firms work with several hundreds of lawyers in their luxurious offices. Advertising agencies like Grey, Ogilvy and BBDO make big money. Vodafone has its European headquarters on a campus in Heerdt – an administrative district on the left side of the Rhine.

It was in Düsseldorf that the

Schlossturm and St. Lambertus

boom of the telecommunication business started: At the end of 1989, Mannesmann won the order to install a telecommunication network D1 is Telekom and D2 stands for Vodafone.

A historical success: it turned out to be a highly profitable idea. Within a few years everybody wanted a mobile phone. Sales shot up, D2 saved weak Mannesmann and became so attractive that, in 1999, British Vodafone fell for D2 and bought Mannesmann after a long takeover battle which was certainly not a marriage of love, more of convenience. Painful for the people of Düsseldorf, the traditional name Mannesmann that had been part of Düsseldorf for many decades and had been employer to thousands of families, had to go. Many feel that the sale was a lesson in global economy.

The mobile city did not suffer in the long run. Many small and bigger

firms connected with the telecommunication business moved in. Today the economic mix is versatile and provides constant tax income – a good base for the financial wellbeing and unique in Germany.

In the new harbour you can touch, feel and see this wealth. In the 1980s, this part of Düsseldorf was full of old cranes and dilapidated factory buildings where cargo ships loaded and unloaded their goods. It has been transformed into a media harbour: the architectural 'wonder' is well known Europe-wide and has often been copied. Many firms connected with media have their offices there, hence the name. But this former industrial harbour is much more. An eating-out culture has developed, so far unknown in Düsseldorf. In the 1980s there were only a few corner pubs waiting for harbour workers; today, top-class restaurants, genuine bistros, small bars and other gastronomic novelties are waiting for costumers. You should find what you're looking for, even fried curry sausage with gold leaves.

Let's have a look at a few of the the star chefs: Jean-Claude Bourgeueil (Enzo im Schiffchen in Kaiserswerth) has two stars from Guide Michelin. Holger Berens (Berens am Kai) has one. A meal at their places means top-class food and there are more gourmet restaurants in and around town.

Düsseldorf's reputation is as colourful as the city itself. Ask three visitors and you'll get three different answers. One will definitely be: Altbier. It's always a correct answer. Nowhere else do you find this beer, it's unique and of a special brew. "Alt" (old) probably refers to the time, when beer was brewed without artificial yeast and refrigeration. Altbier is dark, often very bitter, brewed like English bitter. On the German market Alt is rather exotic, it's drunk in the region of Düsseldorf. Germans in general don't take to it. Düsseldorfers don't mind, they love their beer.

The ESPRIT-Arena on the Rhine

Other typical products? Here you are: Persil, world famous washing powder, comes from Düsseldorf. Löwensenf (mustard) was invented there. Pattex glue from Henkel, too. Less well-known is Killepitsch, a mild bitter which is exported worldwide.

What else? Let's have a look at sports: DEG is the local ice hockey team and most times a much feared opponent. Table tennis stars like Jörg Rosskopf are legendary. Toni Turek was goal keeper in Bern in 1954 and held on to the Hungarian ball. Well remembered is the commentary on the radio: "Toni, you are a football god." He then was the goalkeeper of Fortuna, a club which currently plays second league. And to earn his living he worked as ticket collector at the Rheinbahn.

Several thousands of Japanese people live there, well catered for by Japanese shops, schools and restaurants. People from more than 130 nations live there. Several times a year you can hear all sorts of different languages: a one of the traide fairs is on. Düsseldorf is one of the biggest trade fair centres worldwide, the list is long: Drupa (printing), Kunststoffmesse (plastics), die boot (boats and equipment), Interpack (wrappings), Medica (medicine) and they all are biggest in their line and attract hundreds of thousands of visitors. The visitors of the fairs are part of Düsseldorf, they walk around town, meet locals, and get to know their hectic life on weekdays as well as their leisure lifestyle and their humour.

Hosting the world in Düsseldorf

Events at Düsseldorf trade-fair and exhibition centre or the ESPRIT Arena bring international flair to Düsseldorf. Düsseldorf's trade-fair organisation, today named Messe Düsseldorf GmbH, was originally founded on January 7th ,1947. Today the company organises around 50 trade fairs and events per year and currently employs a staff of more than 1500 worldwide.

Most of the trade-fair and exhibition centre dates back to the year of opening in 1971 and extends over a total area of 305,400 square metres. Every year, around 32,500 exhibitors present their products to almost 2 million visitors in around 19 exhibition halls. Situated right next to the trade-fair and exhibition centre is the ESPRIT-Arena, which opened in January 2005. The Arena can accommodate up to 66,000 spectators or patrons for sports or music events, for example, the Rolling Stones or Madonna.

- ***Messe Düsseldorf GmbH,*** *Messeplatz, Stockumer Kirchstr. 61, Infoline Tel. (02 11) 45 60-900, www.messe-duesseldorf.de*
- ***ESPRIT-Arena,*** *Arena-Str. 1, Tel. (02 11) 15 98 12 00, www.espritarena.de*

But there are other interesting, exciting and leisure attractions in the northern part of Düsseldorf, alongside the major events.

Anyone interested in aquatic animals simply must go to the Aquazoo/ Löbbecke Museum (page 24). Right behind it is the Nordpark with the Japanese Garden (page 45); this park extends as far as the Rhine and offers a peaceful and relaxing atmosphere. If you are looking for more excitement, you can watch the busy flight operations at Düsseldorf International Airport or go shopping there instead.

Düsseldorf trade-fair and exhibition centre

Are you hungry?

- *Excellent cuisine directly on the Rhine:* ***Schnellenburg Restaurant & Hotel,*** *Rotterdamer Straße 120, Tel. (02 11) 4 38 84 38, www.schnellenburg.de, daily 7 am–10.30 am and 12pm–10 pm*
- *Good food in a friendly atmosphere:* ***Café-Restaurant Kastanie,*** *Kaiserswerther Straße 408, Tel. (02 11) 4 36 06 11, www.cafekastanie.de, daily 10 am–1 am*
- *A stylish restaurant offering Greek specialities:* ***Taverna Toxotis,*** *Kaiserswerther Straße 402, Tel. (02 11) 2 00 70 62, www.taverna-toxotis.de, daily 11.30 am–3 pm and 5 pm–11 pm*

Carnival – humour, intrigue and gossiping

Humour? Anything to do with carnival? No, carnival and humour are far from being related. It is far more complicated, humour in the Rhineland is above all a serious matter - carnival guards, associations, societies and clubs draw up standard guide-lines concerning Helau and Rosenmontag (Monday preceding Ash Wednesday/what the carnival parade should look like). Uniforms, swords of honour and medals are proudly worn. It's all a matter of status, influence and pretended importance.

Next to Cologne, Düsseldorf is the centre of carnival, its long and really good Carnival parade on Rosenmontag is prone to breaking records, and each vehicle in the parade has a motto that cynically parodies political or economic problems. There is always a lot of excitement and frustration about the vehicles but in the end they do what they have done right from the beginning: hold the mirror to the established and the powerful and caricature them. Their wit is beyond political correctness.

From residential town to capital of the state

Düsseldorf is not of one mould, it has many faces. Districts have their own traditions; their inhabitants don't feel like Düsseldorfers

Carnival

in the first place, they feel like Kaiserswerther, Bilker or Benrather. That's because of history and its development. In the outskirts of Düsseldorf there were many older towns and settlements of equal rights. No-one quite knows why Düsseldorf got ahead of more powerful towns and villages. Maybe it was the influence of the Counts von Berg who made Düsseldorf a residential town, or maybe it was Jan Wellem who was active in European politics and wanted to have a presentable town. During industrialization Düsseldorf was recognized as a suitable place for industry. Many firms were established and thus Düsseldorf managed to become a city exceeding a population of 100,000 in 1882. In the following years the districts and independent boroughs merged and were incorporated in 1909 and 1929. A few more districts were added during territorial allocations in 1957.

Düsseldorf's role as capital of the federal state of North-Rhine-Westphalia is due to the British, they established their administration site there. But Düsseldorf hasn't lost its atmosphere through this development, it has kept its many faces.

Population

Inhabitants (in total)
(as of 31/12/2013): 597,102
Foreign citizens
(as of 31/12/2012): 109,770
Population density
(as of 31/12/2013):
2,800 inhabitants per km^2

Administrative Data

Administrative district in its own right
Federal state: Nordrhein-Westfalen
Administrative district: Düsseldorf
Regional authority: Rheinland
International sign: D
Postal areas: 40001–40629
Telephone code: 0211
Website: www.duesseldorf.de

Boroughs

Düsseldorf consists of 10 boroughs with 50 districts.
District 1: Altstadt, Carlstadt, Derendorf, Golzheim, Pempelfort, Stadtmitte
District 2: Düsseltal, Flingern-Nord, Flingern-Süd
District 3: Bilk, Flehe, Friedrichstadt, Hafen, Hamm, Oberbilk, Unterbilk, Volmerswerth
District 4: Heerdt, Lörick, Niederkassel, Oberkassel
District 5: Angermund, Kaiserswerth, Kalkum, Lohausen, Stockum, Wittlaer
District 6: Lichtenbroich, Mörsenbroich, Rath, Unterrath
District 7: Gerresheim, Grafenberg, Hubbelrath, Ludenberg, Knittkuhl
District 8: Eller, Lierenfeld, Unterbach, Vennhausen
District 9: Benrath, Hassels, Himmelgeist, Holthausen, Itter, Reisholz, Urdenbach, Wersten
District 10: Garath, Hellerhof

General Facts

Hospitals: 15 (as of 31/12/2006)
Households: 350,816
(as of 31/12/2013)
Hotel beds: 25,216 (as of 31/12/2013
Vehicles: 291,275 (as of 1/1/2014)
Schools: 166 (as of 15/10/2013)
Students: 27,670 (HHU)
(Winter semester13/14)

Geographical Data

It lies 51° 14' 12" north and has a longitude of 06° 48' 39"
City area: 217 km^2
Highest point: Sandberg Hubbelrath 170,3 m above sea level
Highest construction:
Rheinturm, 240.5 m
Highest building:
ARAG-Hochhaus, 124.9 m
Lowest point: Schwarzbach mouth 28.23 m above sea level
Geographical centre point:
Hans-Sachs-Straße at Peter-Janssen-Straße 40
Length of the Rhine in city area: 42.10 km

Partner towns

Chemnitz, Saxony, since 1988
Chongqing, People's Republic of China, since 2004
Haifa, Israel, since 1988
Moscow, Russia, since 1992
Reading, United Kingdom since 1988
Warsaw, Poland, since 1989
Friendly relations since the 1970s with the Norwegian city of **Lillehammer** and since 2003 with the capital of the Balearic Islands, **Palma de Mallorca** (Spain), also with Belgrade in Serbia and Toulouse (France)

Coat of Arms

The original coat of arms was developed when Düsseldorf was proclaimed town in 1288. It shows an anchor which symbolizes the relationship between the township and the Rhine.

When Düsseldorf became a residential capital of the county of Berg, the count created a new coat of arms: a lion with a double tail (heraldic animal of the counts von Berg) holds the anchor in its claws. In the middle of the 18th century this elaborately designed picture replaced the old coat of arms. After various alterations in the 19th and 20th century the added details were removed and in 1938 it got a new, now well-known design: a red lion, upright, with double tail, blue crown and blue arms. He holds a blue dropped anchor.

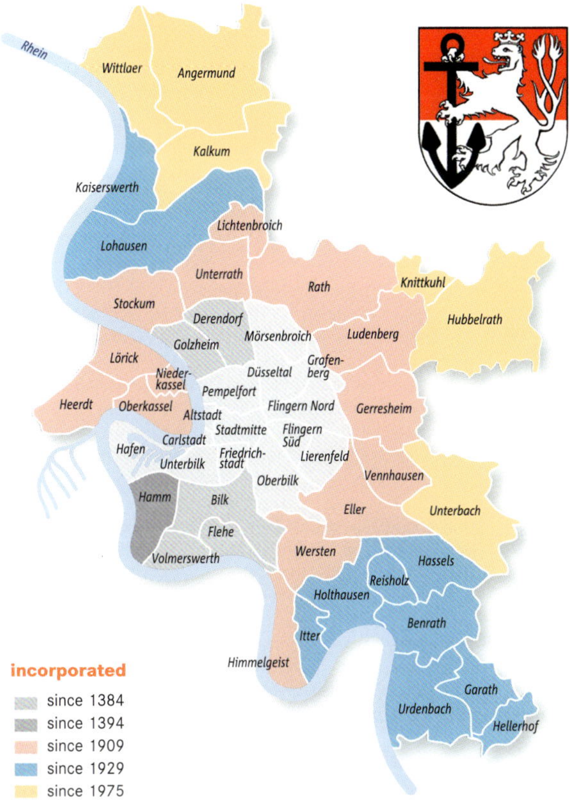

1135	First recorded mention of "Dusseldorp"
1288	After the victory in the battle of Worringen, Count Adolf von Berg proclaims Düsseldorf town
1380	Düsseldorf becomes a Residence
1510	Through the marriage of Maria von Jülich-Berg and Johann von Kleve, Düsseldorf becomes the capital of the united counties.
1545	The first Gymnasium (High School) is founded (today's Görres-Gymnasium)
1570–1573	Rathaus (Town hall) on the Market Place is built
1614	The treaty of Xanten divides the united counties, Brandenburg gets Kleve and Pfalz-Neuenburg gets Jülich and Berg
1679–1716	Government of Johann Wilhelm von Pfalz-Neuenburg, called Jan Wellem
1699	The first regular ferry on the Rhine (Flying Bridge)
1716	After the death of Jan Wellem, his brother Karl Philip transfers the court to Mannheim and thus ends the cultural and economic importance of Düsseldorf
1755–1773	Schloss Benrath is built by Nicolas de Pigage
1762	Schloss Jägerhof by Johann Josef Couven is completed
1771	Nicolas Pigage completes the older part of the court garden
1773	The Kunstakademie is founded
1794–1795	Bombardment and occupation by the French
1797	Heinrich Heine is born in Düsseldorf on December 12th
1801	Retreat of the French occupation
1804	The fortress is destroyed and today's park of the Königsallee and the Heinrich-Heine-Allee is built (by master builder Huschberger and garden architect Weyhe)
1806	Napoleon proclaims Berg a grand county
1811	Napoleon's visit
1815	The Rhineland becomes Prussian
1819	Re-opening of the Academy, Peter Cornelius becomes director. The Academy gains worldwide acknowledgement under his successor Wilhelm von Schadow (1826–1859)
1825	The first carnival parade takes place on the Monday preceding Ash Wednesday
About 1830	Shipping on the Rhine is deregulated
1833–1835	Felix Mendelssohn Bartholdy is municipal Director of music
1848	Foundation of the Malkasten, an artists' association
1850–1854	Robert Schumann is municipal director of music
1870	The first bridge over the Rhine is opened: Hammer Eisenbahnbrücke
1880	Completion of the Ständehaus (seat of the provincial state parliament until 1945 and of the state parliament of North Rhine-Westphalia, 1949–1988)
1882	Düsseldorf becomes a city (more than 100,000 inhabitants)
1896	Opening of the industrial harbour
1898	Opening of the first road bridge over the Rhine (to Oberkassel)
1902	Rhineland-Westphalian exhibition of industry, trade and art
1905	Louise Dumont and Gustav Lindemann founded the Schauspielhaus (playhouse)

1922–1926	Important buildings with influential architectural structures (e.g. Wilhelm-Marx-Haus, Stumm-administration and the administration of the Phoenix AG) are built
1926	First radio station in Düsseldorf, "GeSoLei" (an exhibition of health care, social care and sports), the Ehrenhof is built
1927	The Düsseldorf airport Lohausen is opened
1937	Exhibition of the Third Reich "Schaffendes Volk" (Working people), Nordpark and the Golzheimer Heide are built
1939–1945	During the Second World War Düsseldorf is heavily destroyed and there are more than 5000 deaths among the civilian population
1946	Düsseldorf becomes the capital of the new "Land" North Rhine-Westphalia
1956	Opening of the new opera house
1960	Thyssen skyscraper, called Drei-Scheiben-Haus (the building in three "slices"), is built
1965	Düsseldorf gets a university
1967	Opening of the first S-Bahn (rapid train) (Düsseldorf-Garath/Ratingen)
1970	New Schauspielhaus (theater) is opened
1971	Opening of the Messe (exhibition centre) in the north of Düsseldorf
1972	The Heinrich-Heine prize is given to Carl Zuckmayer for the first time
1973	Beginning of the construction of the subway
1975	Municipal area is divided in 10 districts with own representations
1976	Oberkasseler Brücke is moved 50 metres north
1978	Opening of the Tonhalle
1982	Telecommunication Tower, called Rheinturm (tower of the Rhine), is opened
1985	New central station is officially opened
1986	Opening of the Kunstsammung NRW (art collection North Rhine-Westphalia)
1987	Park in the south is enlarged for the Bundesgartenschau (federal garden exhibition), opening of the Aquazoo/ Löbbecke-Museum
1988	Opening of the Landtag (seat of the state government) at the Rhine, subway starts running
From 1990	Rhine Harbour is rebuilt and becomes 'Medienhafen' (media harbour) with impressive architecture
1993	Promenade along the Rhine and the Filmmuseum are opened
2000	Opening of the biggest fair pavilion in Europe
2001	New Airport opened and Museum Kunstpalast (Palace of Art)
2002	Start of the Garden Show EUROGA 2002 plus in Düsseldorf-Benrath
2004	Opening of LTU-Arena (today's ESPRIT-Arena)
2005	Skyscraper Gap 15 is built
2007	Düsseldorf is free from debt, the media-award BAMBI takes place in the conference centre
from 2009	Redesign of parts of the citycenter including Kö-bogen and expansion of subway
2014	Storm 'Ela' destroys 40,000 trees in the city

CITY OF CULTURE AND ART

Thousands of artists have chosen their domiciles in Düsseldorf. Joseph Beuys worked here and Markus Lüpertz lives here - this is not by chance. The opening of the **Kunstakademie** (Academy of Arts) in the 18th century was the beginning of an intensive and lively art life. It still continues in the numerous museums and galleries and on the small and big stages of the city. Events such as the düsseldorf festival! The Schumannfest (a music festival) or the Jazz Rally are part of the Düsseldorf calendar just as much as literary venues like the Bücherbummel (an exhibition of books) or the lectures in different houses of the city.

The foundation **Museum Kunst Palast** at Ehrenhof on the site of the world's fair exhibition centre of the 1920s is a jewel in the crown among the museums. Close by you'll find the **NRW-Forum** of culture and economy, whose exhibitions focus on photography, design, architecture and media.

Not far away, in the Altstadt, two important museums face each other. There is the **Kunsthalle** whose curator emphasizes young talent and avant-garde art. The elegant black façade opposite belongs to the art collection **K20** that accommodates a world-class exhibition of paintings of the 20th century. Art of the 21st century is a couple of kilometres away in the historical Ständehaus, **K21,** where the North Rhine-Westphalian state representatives sat in the past.

If you want to learn more about the history of Düsseldorf you should visit the **Stadtmuseum** - from there it's only a few steps to the **Film Museum** and the **Hetjens-Museum**/Deutsches Keramikmuseum (German museum of ceramics) in the Alter Hafen (a former inner harbour). It is the only German museum that specializes in artfully created and important ceramic objects. Two other museums focus on flora and fauna: The **Aquazoo/Löbbecke-Museum** at Nordpark and the **Museum für europäische Gartenkunst** (Museum of European Garden Art) in the Schloss Benrath.

Should you feel like going to a cabaret, good theatre or concerts - or should you prefer to relax with comedy or jazz - no problem, Düsseldorf's rich scene offers something for everyone's taste. There are not only the **Deutsche Oper am Rhein** (opera), the **Schauspielhaus** (Gustaf Gründgens used to be one of the directors of this theatre) or the concert hall **Tonhalle** but also a lot of smaller places to go to. The **Theater an der Kö** and the **Komödie** are first choice among the boulevard theatres.

There are glamorous shows in the old tram depot – today's **Capitol Theater** for musicals – or in the **Apollo-Varieté**. Bernhard Paul, the owner of the Roncalli circus chooses the artists. A visit is worthwhile for the astonishing architecture. The cabaret

A concert in the Tonhalle

K21 – the modern art collection

Kom(m)ödchen has had an outstanding reputation throughout Germany since its foundation by Kay and Lore Lorentz shortly after the Second World War.

Not only the Kom(m)ödchen, the **Savoy Theater,** an old cinema, also offers cabaret at its best together with good music. Dieter Hildebrandt and Konrad Beikircher, the well-known Rhinelander from South Tyrol, perform there. Jazz specialists play in the old forge, called **Jazzschmiede,** in an old industrial area. **Robert-Schumann-Musikhochschule** (school of music) regularly opens its doors to the public.

The small theatres in different quarters like **Flin** in Ludenberg or the **Theater an der Luegallee** in Oberkassel attract audiences because of their homely and cosy atmosphere. Should you be more interested in fringe theatre then you should study the programmes of the two **FFT** theatres. FFT stands for forum of the free theatres: groups from all over Germany and abroad perform on a high level. Keen on dancing, go to the **Tanzhaus NRW** (dance hall) you might even try a few steps.

Literature and film

Who would not praise Heinrich Heine? But is anybody going to read him? Standing in his shadow Friedrich Spee von Langenfeld from Kaiserswerth (1591–1635), poet, theologist and critic. He caused a stir with his poems "Trutz Nachtigall" and his polemic against witch hunts ("Cautio Criminalis"). After Heine, things were quiet. The town of Düsseldorf and the political circumstances didn't care much about poets and dramatists like Karl Immermann and Christian Grabbe. "Jokes, satire, irony and deeper meanings" didn't mean much to the Düsseldorfers. It was the 20th century that brought some success.

Hanns Heinz Ewers (1871–1943) published two novels "Der Student von Prag" (The student of Prague) and "Alraune" (Mandrake), both were hits and films were made from them several times. He joined the National Socialist party in 1933 and was in favour of a monument for Heine - very peculiar. Let's turn to Hermann Harry Schmitz (1880–1913), a satirist who didn't match the standard of Tucholsky or Karl Kraus but managed to get under middle class skins. And let's mention Heinrich Spoerl's "Feuerzangenbowle" (the name of a type of hot rum punch). Günter Grass in his "Tin Drum" did it and Dieter Forte (*1935) in his novels did it even more drastically: tell about this city and its history, about youth, war and suffering in Düsseldorf, especially in Oberbilk. Thomas Kling, poet, died in 2005. He belonged to the pub scene with an impressive play on words. He was definitely outshone by Rose Ausländer, a poet born in 1907 in Czernowitz. She died in Düsseldorf in 1988.

Film directors often left Düsseldorf in a hurry because of a lack of infrastructure. But when talking about the film history of Düsseldorf, Ludwig Gottschalk has to be mentioned; he bought "Fate and Passion" by Asta Nielsen in Copenhagen. He didn't resell it by the metre as it was the custom in those days but distributed it. That was the beginning of Düsseldorf's importance as a film distributors' city. The twenty-year-old Harry Piel from Benrath became famous beyond German borders. He was an actor, a director and a stuntman - in exciting films with animals of prey - in one person. Helmut Käutner, a German film virtuoso with French elegance, was blanked out by the Nazis. His film "Great Freedom #7" was also banned. The most important titles of his films are: "Romance in a Minor Key", "Under the Bridges", "Ludwig II", "Devil's General". In 1960 he made the hilarious comedy "A Glass of Water" with Gustaf Gründgens, also born in Düsseldorf, and Lilo Pulver. "Der große GG" (the big Gustaf Gründgens) was already on the screen as a gang boss in "M" by Fritz Lang or in "Liebelei: a tragedy of love and lost honour" by Max Opüls where he was exactly as "aasig" (diabolic) as he was said to be.

Wim Wenders, on the other hand, born in Klever Straße in 1945, achieved international fame relatively easily: Paris, Munich, festivals and successful films ("Paris, Texas"). He won't mind if we mention some of those who stayed at home. Lutz Mommart, his outstanding minimalist short films "Zero" and "Flux" and also his films like "Tango durch Deutschland". A whole generation of experimental filmmakers came from the Kunstakademie: Kaminski, Neddermann, Schlingmann, Huy and Sacks.

Hard to classify: The overwhelming cartoon maker Viktor Boiko (who died in 2008) and Philip Gröning, the film director of films and documentaries from Lohhausen.

TIPS

Stadtmuseum

The Museum of the History of Düsseldorf is itself historical; it is 130 years old and the oldest museum in the city. In the sixties it was moved to the Palais Spee. It shows a permanent exhibition from early history until today as well as changing exhibitions on various aspects of the city's history.

- ***Carlstadt,*** *Berger Allee 2, Tel. (02 11) 8 99 61 70, Tue–Sun 11am–6pm, www.duesseldorf.de/stadtmuseum*

K20

The art collection rebuilt in 2010 has a renowned place in the international museum scene with its works of west European and American modern art. The art collection shows outstanding works from Pablo Picasso to Joseph Beuys. With spectacular exhibitions you'll face long queues.

- ***Altstadt,*** *Grabbeplatz 5, Tel. (02 11) 83 81-130, Tue–Fri 10am–6pm, Sat/Sun/public holidays 11am–6pm, first Wednesday 10am–10pm, www.kunstsammlung.de*

Capitol Theater

The musical theatre is situated in a former tram depot. Successful musicals like "Cats" and "Saturday Night Fever" have been performed in the big hall with 1,250 seats.

- ***Flingern,*** *Erkrather Str. 30, Tel. (02 11) 7 34 41 50, www.capitol-theater.de*

Aquazoo/Löbbecke Museum

MUSEUMS

Aquazoo/Löbbecke Museum

500 animals can be seen in the aquariums and terrariums. The base of the museum is the natural historical collection of Theodor Löbbecke, a scientist and pharmacist from the 19th century.

- ***Golzheim,*** *Kaiserswerther Str. 380, Tel. (02 11) 8 99 61 50, currently closed for renovation www.duesseldorf.de/aquazoo*

Filmmuseum

This museum has national importance; only four collections of films exist. The history and the technique of films are well presented. One of the attractions is a studio with camera, light techniques, wind machines etc. and a cinematic studio

("Black Box"). Special exhibitions deal with films, cinemas und stars.

▮ ***Carlstadt,*** *Schulstr. 4, Tel. (02 11) 8 99 22 32, Tue–Sun 11am–5pm Wed 11am–9pm, www.duesseldorf.de/filmmuseum*

Glasmuseum Hentrich

The Hentrich collection of glass, after the Victoria & Albert Museum in London, is the most comprehensive one in Europe. It shows the development of luxurious glass from the pre-Roman period to the studio glass of modern times. The heart of the collection are the precious pieces owned by the architect Helmut Hentrich.

▮ ***Pempelfort,*** *Ehrenhof 4–5, Tel. (02 11) 8 99 24 63, Tue–Sun 11am–6pm, Thu 11am–9pm, www.museum-kunst-palast.de*

Art collection K 20 at Grabbeplatz

Goethe-Museum

Goethe was in Düsseldorf from 1774 to 1792 and stayed in the Künstlerhaus Malkasten (artists' home called paintbox). Next door, in the castle Jägerhof is today's Goethe museum. It deals with the life and work of the poet. Precious manuscripts, letters, drawings, paintings, busts as well as documents of Goethe's Theory of Colours. In the library you'll find first editions.

▮ ***Pempelfort,*** *Jacobistr. 2, Tel. (02 11) 8 99 62 62, Tue–Fri/ Sun 11am–5pm, Sat 1pm–5pm, www.goethe-museum.com*

Hetjens-Museum

When, in 1906, the collector Laurent Heinrich Hetjens gave his valuable ceramics to his birth town, he did it on condition that a museum was built for it. In 1909 the only worldwide institute was opened. The universal history of ceramics from its beginning 8,000 years ago to these days is represented in the Palace Nesselrode.

▮ ***Carlstadt,*** *Schulstr. 4, Tel. (02 11) 8 99 42 10, Tue–Sun 11am–5pm, Wed 11am–9pm, www.duesseldorf.de/hetjens*

K21

The art collection shows international art from 1980 onwards in the former seat of the NRW state parliament in the Ständehaus. Specific starting points of the sixties and seventies are outlined through important works of Marcel Broodhaers and Nam June Paik. In July 2004 the young museum was considerably expanded with the Ackermann collection.

- ***Unterbilk,*** *Ständehausstr. 1, Tel. (02 11) 83 81-600, Tue–Fri 10am–6pm, Sat/Sun/public holidays 11am–6pm, first Wednesday 10am–10pm, www.kunstsammlung.de*

Kunsthalle

This concrete-cube, made of prefabricated parts, was built in 1967 and is a rare example of brutalist architecture in Düsseldorf. The Kunsthalle and the Kunstverein für die Rheinlande und Westfalen are there. As an institution for changing exhibitions without its own collection, the Kunsthalle focuses on contemporary art and its historical and local references.

- ***Altstadt,*** *Grabbeplatz 4, Tel. (02 11) 8 99 62 43, Tue–Sun/public holidays 11am–6pm, last Thursday 11am-8pm, www.kunsthalle-duesseldorf.de*

Museum für Gartenkunst

The East wing of Schloss Benrath got a worldwide unique exhibition in 41 rooms. The history of garden art from the antiquity to today can be explored during four tours. The main emphasis is on the prime period of the 17th and 19th century. A virtual stroll through Düsseldorf and its garden is a special attraction.

- ***Benrath,*** *Benrather Schlossallee 100–106, Tel. (02 11) 8 99 38 32, April 16th–Oct 31st Tue–Sun 10am–6pm, Nov 1st–April 15th Tue–Sun 11am–5pm, www.schloss-benrath.de*

Museum für Naturkunde

In the West wing of Schloss Benrath you'll find an exhibition that deals with the natural history of the Niederrheinische Bucht (Lower Rhine Bay) and Niederbergisches Land (a hilly area east of Düsseldorf). It starts with flora and fauna of the castle park. The Benrather Vogeluhr (a birds' clock) with the morning songs of the breeding birds in the park is a big attraction.

- ***Benrath,*** *Benrather Schlossallee 100–106, Tel. (02 11) 8 99 38 32 April 1th–Oct 31st Tue–Fri 11am–5pm, Sat/Sun 11am-6pm, Nov 1st–March31st ,Tue–Sun 11am–5pm, www.schloss-benrath.de*

Museum Kunstpalast

As the city had no money for the restoration of the museum they chose a public-private-partnership. With a trust sponsored by E.ON, an electricity company, and other partners they managed to restore the museum und the Robert Schumann concert hall which is a first choice for concerts.

- ***Pempelfort,*** *Ehrenhof 4–5, Tel. (02 11) 8 99 24 60, Tue–Sun 11am–6pm, Thu 11am–6pm, www.museum-kunst-palast.de*

NRW-Forum

Young visitors especially are interested in the exhibitions about photography, media, fashion, communication, mobility and lifestyle.

- ***Pempelfort,*** *Ehrenhof 2, Tel. (02 11) 8 92 66 81, Tue–Sun 11am–8pm, Fri 11am-10pm www.nrw-forum.de*

The Schlossturm with the Schifffahrtmuseum

SchifffahrtMuseum

The home of the shipping museum is the symbol of Düsseldorf: the Schlossturm from the 14th century near the Rhine. Facts about the life on and with the Rhine from the Romans until today are shown. The ship models are very attractive. A multi media show explains the history of Düsseldorf.

- ***Altstadt,*** *Burgplatz 30, Tel. (02 11) 8 99 41 95, Tue–Sun 11am–6pm, www.freunde-schifffahrtmuseum.de*

Theatermuseum

Start your theatre evening here: The permanent exhibition Schau-Plätze in the former house of the court gardener informs you about the different periods of theatre history in Germany, especially in Düsseldorf – starting with the court theatre in the 16th century up to Gustaf Gründgens and his successors. Changing exhibitions present famous persons.

- ***Pempelfort,*** *Jägerhofstr. 1, Tel. (02 11) 8 99 61 30, Tue–Sun 1pm–7pm, www.duesseldorf.de/theatermuseum*

THEATRES

Apollo Varieté

At the beginning of the century there was a variety theatre by this name on the Kö and the founder of the Roncalli Circus continues with this tradition under the Kniebrücke. He shows artistry, acrobatics, clownery and magic. The programme changes every three months and you can enjoy the performances sitting at little tables.

- ***Unterbilk,*** *Apollo Platz 1, Tel. (02 11) 8 28 90 90, www.apollo-variete.com*

Deutsche Oper am Rhein

Deutsche Oper am Rhein is the name of the two operas Duisburg and Düsseldorf. Its ensemble has a first class reputation in Germany and offers a wide repertoire of classical and new opera as well as excellent ballet performances. The historical auditorium from the 19th century was destroyed during the Second World War. It was rebuilt in 1954–56 and since then it looks rather functional and bare.

- ***Stadtmitte,*** *Heinrich-Heine-Allee 16a, Tel. (02 11) 8 90 80, tickets 8 92 52 11, www.rheinoper.de*

Komödie

Ingrid Braut and Alfons Höckmann opened the theatre in August 1968. Today's directors are Helmuth Fuschl and Paul Haizmann from Vienna. They show light boulevard theatre in modern productions, classics like "Feuerzangenbowle" (the name of a hot rum punch) as well as modern works.

- ***Stadtmitte,*** *Steinstr. 23, Tel. (02 11) 13 37 07 and 32 51 51, www. komoedie-steinstrasse.de*

Kom(m)ödchen

At the beginning of the political-literary cabaret there was a couple: Kay and Lore Lorentz celebrated the first night of their Kom(m) ödchen with the programme "Positively against it ..." in 1947. Their son, Kay Sebastian Lorentz, successfully led the theatre into a new era.

- ***Altstadt,*** *Kay-und-Lore-Lorentz-Platz, tickets Tel. (02 11) 32 94 43, www.kommoedchen.de*

Marionetten-Theater

The puppet theatre was newly founded in 1985 by Anton Bachleitner. The repertoire includes 22 full-length productions. "Krabat" by Ottfried Preußler is for children, but most of the productions like the philosophical "Sternstunde" (great moment) appeals to adults.

- ***Carlstadt,*** *Palais Wittgenstein Bilker Str. 7, Tel. (02 11) 32 84 32 www.marionettentheater-duesseldorf.de*

Puppentheater Helmholtzstraße

A lot of fun for the very small ones: some of the performances are suitable for two-year-old kids. Parents also are welcome but they have to sit at the back so that the little ones can see well. You can be sure, as soon as the curtain rises, everybody will calm down and follow the lovely productions.

- ***Friedrichstadt,*** *Helmholtzstr. 38, Tel. (02 11) 37 24 01, www.puppentheater.de*

Savoy Theater

The time of the big cinemas in the city is over. The Savoy theatre has been lucky. Concert Agent Stefan Jürging re-opened the cinema originally from the fifties in 2000 and installed a stage for artists like Ulrich Tukur. The programme includes cabaret, variety and concerts and there is a cinema in the basement.

- ***Friedrichstadt,*** *Graf-Adolf-Str. 47, Tel. (02 11) 8 30 89 00, www.savoy-theater.de*

At the Marionettentheater

Schauspielhaus Düsseldorf

Schauspielhaus

The curved design of the theater is a Düsseldorf landmark. There are two stages behind the façade, the big auditorium with 900 seats and the small auditorium with 300 seats. Junges Schauspielhaus (young theater) shows productions for younger people. Studio Central offers unconventional plays by German and international actors.

- ***Stadtmitte,*** *Gustaf-Gründgens-Platz 1, Tel. tickets (02 11) 36 99 11, www.duesseldorfer-schauspielhaus.de*
- ***Stadtmitte,*** *Studio Central in der Alten Paketpost, Worringer Str. 140, Tel. tickets (02 11) 36 99 11, www.duesseldorfer-schauspielhaus.de*
- ***Mörsenbroich,*** *Junges Schauspielhaus, Münsterstr. 446, Tel. tickets (02 11) 8 52 37 11, www.junges-schauspielhaus.de*

Theater an der Kö

You want to see famous German TV personalities? Go to the theatre on the Kö. Gudrun Landgrebe, Martin Semmelrogge and Anja Kruse were on stage here. There are guest performances of cabaret and comedy.

- ***Stadtmitte,*** *Schadow-Arkaden, Tel. (02 11) 32 23 33, www.theateranderkoe.de*

LITERATURE

Heine-Haus

Heine-Haus occupies a historical place in the middle of the old town: Heinrich Heine was born there in 1797. The house was opened on February 17th 2006, the day he died 150 years before. The building houses the Müller & Böhm bookshop and a well-restored lecture hall. Matinees on Sundays and readings take place there.

- ***Altstadt,*** *Bolkerstr. 53, Tel. (02 11) 3 11 25 22, www.heinehaus.de*

MUSIC

Alte Schmiede (Jazzschmiede)

The Alte Schmiede (The Old Forge) is part of a renovated factory, the Salzmann building, and it is one of the most beautiful concert halls of Düsseldorf: The acoustics are overwhelming and it has an excellent grand piano. You can listen to jazz played by young musicians of the area. The jazz club Düsseldorf organizes jam sessions so that young people meet. Jazz players from all over the world perform in special concerts.

- ***Bilk,*** *Himmelgeister Str. 107g, Tel. (02 11) 3 11 05 64, www.jazz-schmiede.de*

Palais Wittgenstein

Not far from the weekly market on Carlsplatz is the municipal cultural centre Palais Wittgenstein. In the chamber music hall, there are concerts of different styles, also with young unknown artists.

- ***Carlstadt,*** *Bilker Str. 7–9, Tel. (02 11) 8 99 61 09*

Mitsubishi Electric Hall

Artists who attract thousands of fans perform in this large hall. Udo Jürgens, BAP and Tokio Hotel were here. There are around 1000 parking spaces subject to charge in the car park. Bus and tram are recommended.

- ***Oberbilk,*** *Siegburger Str. 15, Tel. (02 11) 77 50 57, www.mitsubishi-electric-halle.de*

Robert-Schumann-Saal

The Robert-Schumann-Hall is a multifunctional chamber music hall integrated into the Museum Kunstpalast in Ehrenhof. The Hall has 1,000 square metres with 830 seats. On the programme you'll find various concerts: chamber music, jazz, folk, gospel and world music as well as cabaret and lectures.

- ***Pempelfort,*** *Ehrenhof 4–5, Tel. (02 11) 8 99 24 50, www.robert-schumann-saal.de*

Tonhalle

The impressive hemispherical building on the Rhine was once a planetarium. In the 1970s the architect Helmut Hentrich transformed it into a concert hall. In 2005 the concert hall was extensively modernized and now satisfies the highest standards

Tonhalle - home of the symphonic orchestra

Church Music

Johanneskantorei/Johanneskirche

The choir of the Johanneskirche gives concerts in their church. It has got 90 members, all very fond of church music. They perform demanding choral music from the Renaissance to modern times. The Protestant church also offers other concerts, jazz and organ music.

▮ ***Stadtmitte,*** *Martin Luther-Platz 39, Tel. (02 11) 13 58 10, www.johanneskantorei-duesseldorf.de, www.johanneskirche.org*

Neanderkirche

Regular jazz services are performed in the "Jazzchurch", a Protestant church in the old town. The Neander choir performs as well and during summer the Neander church organizes a series of "Sommerliche Orgelkonzerte" (summer organ concerts).

▮ ***Altstadt,*** *Bolkertsr. 36, Tel. (02 11) 8 36 99 21, www.neandermusik.de, www.neanderkirche.de*

St. Lambertus

Lambertus Church with its lopsided tower is one of the most conspicuous churches of Düsseldorf. Regular choir and organ concerts take place: the Stift Choir founded in 1876 has about 60 members, its repertoire includes the old masters and modern composers.

▮ ***Altstadt,*** *Stiftsplatz 7, Tel. (02 11) 13 23 26, www.lambertuskirche.de*

St. Maximilian

In the traditional Catholic church St. Maximilian in the old town, lovingly called "die Max", music plays an important role. The Maxchoir and the orchestra regularly perform festive High Mass and the organ player and well-known soloists give many concerts. Every Saturday at 11.30pm half an hour of organ music is played "Orgelmusik zur Marktzeit (Organ music at market time).

▮ ***Altstadt,*** *Citadellstr. 2a, Tel. (02 11) 13 16 60 , www.maxkirche.de*

Johanneskirche

of musical performance. It is the home of the Düsseldorf symphony orchestra which has an outstanding reputation.

- ***Pempelfort,*** *Ehrenhof 1, concert box office Tel. (02 11) 8 99 61 23, Mon–Fri 10am–7pm, Sat 10am–2pm, evening box office one hour before the concerts start, www.tonhalle.de*

CINEMAS

Bambi

This independent cinema from 1965 is the oldest in Düsseldorf. It has two screens with 138 and 78 seats and shows many premieres. In recent years Bambi has received many prizes for its exceptional programme.

- ***Stadtmitte,*** *Klosterstr. 78, Tel. (02 11) 35 36 35, www.filmkunstkinos.de*

Cinema

The traditional cinema is famous for its excellent premiere programme. Before or after the cinema the visitors can visit the cosy cinema café. The cinema is well-known for its gala openings with an accompanying programe and specialities according to the film.

- ***Altstadt,*** *Schneider-Wibbel-Gasse 5–7, Tel. (02 11) 8 36 99 72, www.filmkunstkinos.de*

Metropol

This cinema, situated right in the middle of the student district, is very popular with young people especially. It has a rich and varied programme and frequently offers film nights and live music.

- ***Bilk,*** *Brunnenstr. 20, Tel. (02 11) 34 97 09, www.filmkunstkinos.de*

Souterrain

The cosy sitting room cinema in the basement of the restaurant Muggel is unique: the small cinema can hold only 60 persons, and the projectionist is responsible for the bar, which is also open during the film. The varied programme is exclusive with the odd gem.

- ***Oberkassel,*** *Dominikanerstr. 4, Tel. (02 11) 5 57 18 31, www.filmkunstkinos.de*

UCI Kinowelt

Nine screens with the latest films for about 2,800 cinema fans in this modern multiplex cinema. Events with laser shows and film stars on their premiere tours. Several snack bars, bars and a restaurant.

- ***Hafen,*** *Hammer Str. 29–31, Tel. (02 11) 30 08 53 85, www.uci-kinowelt.de*

UFA Filmpalast

This multiplex cinema was the first in town: twelve screens with room for 2,850 visitors, accessible for wheel-chair users. On the top floor blockbuster fans have a good time. In the art house on the ground floor you'll find high quality films and family programmes.

- ***Stadtmitte,*** *Worringer Str. 142, Tel. (02 11) 6 30 67 02, tickets (01 80) 5 05 06 66, www.ufa-duesseldorf.de*

Commerz Real Cinema at Rhine water front

OPEN AIR CINEMA EVENTS

Commerz Real Cinema

View of the Rhine and a 400 square-metre screen – supposedly the biggest hydraulic screen worldwide with film premieres, previews and new films. You can't bring your food and drinks along but bars serve food and drinks. In case of rain, red plastic ponchos are provided.

▪ ***Pempelfort,*** *Robert-Lehr-Ufer, www.commerzrealcinema.de*

Vier Linden Open Air

In nice weather only the screen is opened in the secluded beer garden. In a romantic atmosphere, you can enjoy art cinema programmes. You can bring your food for barbecue and your drinks for cooling.

▪ ***Oberbilk,*** *Siegburger Str. 25, Tel. (02 11) 7 21 31 34, Tue/Thu/Fri/Sat from 9.30pm, www.filmkunstkinos.de*

LEISURE TIME

Düsseldorf has a lot to offer: it is well known as a centre for fashion; it has got "the world's longest bar" and numerous museums. Gardens, parks landscape and nature reserves are ideal for walking. The **Hofgarten** is the most popular park in Düsseldorf and offers great art, like "Reclining Figure in two parts" by Henry Moore in front of the opera, illuminated benches in the Jägerhof Allee or the fountain "Jröner Jong" (green boy).
Nordpark is famous for its beautifull flowers and the water garden. It was developed for the exhibition "Schaffendes Volk" (working people) in 1937. Visit the **Japanischer Garten** as well as the Aquazoo, the exhibition centre Ballhaus and the café (Entrance Kaiserswerther Str. 390).

Volksgarten and **Südpark** are very popular with families in the summer. The south entrance connects with the **Botanischer Garten** of the university: a round hall with tropical plants attracts the public.

The garden administration of the city of Düsseldorf offers 55 guided tours for those who love nature. The popular tours include nature reserves, historical parks, forests and cemeteries. Those interested will also have the opportunity to see Hofgarten as well as **Lantz'schen Park** and **Zoopark**. The tours go along **Aaper Wald** (forest), **Kalkumer** and **Hasseler Forst.**

Just outside Düsseldorf is the large recreation park Volkardey with **Grüner See** (lake), swimming is not allowed. You can go sailing, canoeing, rowing and fishing on **Unterbacher See,** surrounded by woods. There are two beaches for swimming. Though intensively used for leisure activities, the lakes are a wild bird refuge for water birds: nearly 60 species are to be found there. Four islands are declared a bird refuge for swans, Eurasian coots, greylag geese and Canadian geese. A popular place for family outings is **Kaarster See** on the outskirts of Düsseldorf. It's good for swimming – shallow water for those who can't swim, low banks, and a playground attract children. **Blauer See** in Ratingen offers substantial leisure activities, from fairytale zoo to pony riding.

There are two wellness temples in Düsseldorf to help you relax: **Münstertherme,** renovated in 2003; classical ambience in art deco and from the 1870s (Gründerzeit) and the new Sauna in Benrath.

Düsseldorf is well known throughout the region for its events. Highlights are the **Bücherbummel** along Kö which attracts hundreds of thousands of bookworms every year and the largest **fun fair** along the Rhine. Every year, in the third week of July more than 300 brand new and traditional fun fair rides attract millions of people. Important highlight is the huge fireworks.

Hofgarten

CITY OF SPORTS

Düsseldorf seemed a lost cause for sport: the **DEG** ice-hockey team, Fortuna football team and handball team had all hit bottom and seemed to have lost all importance. Now they are back on the sporting stage and making all of Germany aware of Düsseldorf. But Düsseldorf does not just offer classics like football, handball and hockey: world class tennis in Rochusclub and first-class table tennis at Staufenplatz or the hunt for the basketball at the Giants – the choice is enormous.

For South Americans Düsseldorf means fashion and tennis – the latter is most important for Chileans. Players Nicolas Massu and Fernando Gonzalez made history in Rochusclub. They won the first world champion title for Chile at the Arag World Team Cup, later called Düsseldorf Open, which was carried out at Rolander Weg until 2014.

A stone's throw away is the home of a club that brings about champions: **Borussia Düsseldorf** with players like Eberhard Schöler, Jörg Roßkopf or Steffen Fetzner, Timo Boll and Christian Süß – all names that stand worldwide for world-class table tennis. But the managers in the background are not patting themselves on the back. Borussia Düsseldorf is home of the German table tennis centre – they will be on the safe side with up-and-coming players.

For decades, the zoo district was the pinnacle of happines for ice hockey in the Rhineland region. Eight championships gave cause for celebration, and one relegation resulted in a fall back into mediocrity. But that's all over now. The future lies in the Dome stadium in Rath, built for around 70 million euros, where the DEG would like to regain its former glory.

The last station of the journey through the sports city is Flinger Broich; a place which doesn't fit into fashionable Düsseldorf. Nobody wears Prada or Gucci, you wear red and white, the colours of **Fortuna Düsseldorf.** You love the football club or you hate it. If you love it you must know how to suffer. Recent years have been hard with many ups and downs, on the whole far more downs than ups. But this club has got a new home, too. ESPRIT-Arena stands for first class football and lots of applause. There is life in the old team yet.

SPORTS

American football

The Panthers is Germany's oldest still-existing American Football Club.

▪ ***Stockum,*** *Düsseldorf Panther, Kleine Kampfbahn at Arena-Sportpark, Stockumer Höfe, www.duesseldorfpanther.de*

Basketball

Basketball as a leisure activity is becoming increasingly popular among young people. The Giants are hoping to gain points for the league table and even more fans. The team plays in the new sports centre in Burg-Wächter Castello – also the training site of the HSG handball players.

- ***Reisholz,*** *Karl-Hohmann-Str. 1, Tel. (02 11) 90 48 55 81, www.duesseldorfmagics.com*

Bowling

In the USA bowling is a well known sport and often seen on TV. In Germany it is more a leisure activity. If you want to go bowling in Düsseldorf you'll have to go to the bowling centres, often clubs requiring membership. For skittle fans it is far easier, they find a skittle alley in every second pub. Düsseldorf BV (bowling club) practices on the bowling alley in Benrath whereas the bowling alley of Cosmo-Sport is for the whole family.

- ***Benrath,*** *Bowling-Zentrum Düsseldorf, Wimpfener Str. 18, Tel. (02 11) 7 18 29 74, Mon–Thu 5pm–10pm, Fri 5pm–12am, Sat 2pm–12am, Sun 11am–8pm*
- ***Gerresheim,*** *Cosmo-Bowling, Diepenstr. 83, Tel. (02 11) 2 39 57 30, Mon–Thu/Sun 10am–12am Fri/Sat 10–1am, www.cosmo-bowling.de*

Climbing

The Rhineland is flat and climbing fans have to use artificial possibilities. Several halls compete for visitors. Climbing in Heerdt is a nice alternative: a factory hall became an area of more than 800 square metres for climbing. If you need a rest, there's a bistro in the middle of the hall.

TIPS

Concerts in Hofgarten

Summers are full of music in Hofgarten. Concerts take place at the Musikpavillon near Reitallee almost every Sunday. The events start at 11am and last one hour.

- ***Stadtmitte/Pempelfort,*** *Musikpavillon at Hofgarten, Sun 11am–12p, May till Sep*

Golf

Golf has a long tradition in Düsseldorf. The German Open was played several times on the golf course of Hubbelrath club. And, at the junior championship in Hubbelrath, the club's own junior players did well. With two courses the Hubbelrath course meets the expectations of a modern golf course.

- ***Hafen,*** *Golf-Sport-Verein Düsseldorf, Auf der Lausward 51, Tel. (02 11) 41 05 29, www.gsvgolf.de*
- ***Hubbelrath,*** *GC Hubbelrath Bergische Landstr. 700, Tel. (0 21 04) 7 21 78, www.gc-hubbelrath.de*

Skiing

Thanks to the skiing hall in Neuss ski addicts can enjoy skiing all year round. A 300 meter run and a constant temperature of 4 degrees below zero shortens the time till the winter holidays.

- ***Neuss,*** *An der Skihalle 1, Tel. (0 21 31) 1 24 40, Oct 1st–April 30th, Sun-Thu 9am-10pm, Fri/Sa 9am-10.30pm May 1st–Sept 30th, Sun-Thu 9.30am-10pm, Fri/Sat 9.30am-10.30pm, www.allrounder.de*

- ***Gerresheim,*** *Vertical Park, Diepenstr. 83, Tel. (02 11) 29 93 62, Tue–Fri 3pm–11pm (Apr–Sept 6pm–11pm), Sat/Sun 10am–10pm, (Apr-Sept 12am-10pm) www.vertical-park.de*
- ***Heerdt,*** *Klettermassiv, Wiesenstr. 76, Tel. (02 11) 5 63 87 89, Mon 5pm–11pm, Tue–Fri 3pm–11pm, Sat/Sun 11am–8pm, www.klettermassiv.de*

Cycling

Once a year, the traditional cycle race "Round the Kö" attracts cyclists from different European countries. Famous competitor of recent years was Sven Teutenberg. He opened the cycle shop La Bici in Düsseldorf, a place cyclists meet to go on cycling tours.

- ***Stadtmitte,*** *Round the Kö 2015 is organised by three clubs, e. g. www.radsport-aliens-duesseldorf.de*
- ***Oberkassel,*** *La Bici, Leostr. 2, Tel. (02 11) 1 71 54 23, www.labici.de*

DEG (Düsseldorf ice hockey club)

In summer 2006 a new era began for one of the most traditional German ice hockey clubs. Düsseldorf club DEG left the run-down but much loved ice rink at Brehmstraße and moved to the new ISS Dome in Rath. This was meant to be the final step towards winning the championship again. At the end of the 90s the club was relegated to the second league. By now the red-yellow players are determined to stay in the first league and win. Their chances are good considering their substantial financial possibilities. All they need is to transfer emotions and enthusiasm into the new dome and then a DEG match will once more stand for substantial performance.

- ***Rath,*** *ISS Dome, Theodorstr. 281, office Brehmstr. 27a, Tel. (02 11) 86 32 59-0, www.deg-eishockey.de*

Cycling at the Rhine water front

Diving

You can dive in the warm Mediterranean and in Düsseldorf as well. Indoor pools offer special training sessions and hobby divers can dive in various lakes like Elbsee. Taster sessions at a very low price or for free help you find out whether you really like it.

- ***Eller,*** *Tiefenrausch e.V., Training im Schwimmbad am Kikweg, Heidelberger Str. 75, Tel. (02 11) 7 48 08 29 Sun 11am–12pm, www.tiefenrausch-ev.de*
- ***Stockum,*** *Scuba Libre e.V., training at Rheinbad, Europaplatz 1, Tel. (01 77) 4 48 44 86, Wed 7.45-9.30pm, www.scuba-libre.de*

Fortuna (footballteam)

Although they were at one stage relegated to the fourth league – apart from the DEG, Fortuna is the most popular sports club in Düsseldorf. Even when the number of spectators was at its lowest, the love-hate relationship with the football players from Flingern was a topic in pubs and cafés. Meanwhile Fortuna has gained popularity, especially among young people due to their cooperation with Die Toten Hosen, a very popular German punk band. The number of spectators at the ESPRIT-Arena has gone up – not only since they've played in the 2nd league.

- ***Stockum,*** *ESPRIT-Arena, Arena-Str. 1 and Paul-Janes-Stadion, office Flinger Broich 87, Tel. (02 11) 23 80 10, www.fortuna-duesseldorf.de*

Gyms

If you feel like working out indoors or enjoying a day in a spa, there are several gyms in town with modern equipment and skilled staff to assist you. Day passes are available for non-members.

- ***City Centre,*** *Fitness First, Schadowstr. 17/21 (Schadow-Arkaden), Tel. (02 11) 8 28 53 80 www.fitnessfirst.de*
- ***City Centre,*** *Holmes Place, Königsallee 59, Tel. (02 11) 64 97 00 00, www.holmesplace.de*

Ice sports

Ice skating fans get what they want in Düsseldorf: there are two ice rinks with long opening hours. In the old ice rink at Brehmstraße you can feel the atmosphere of many championships. Benrath ice rink is never really crowded, ideal for beginners.

- ***Benrath,*** *Eissporthalle Benrath, Paulsmühlenstr. 6, Tel. (02 11) 71 59 59, Mon–Sat 2pm–4pm and 5pm–7pm, Tue/Fri 9am–1pm, Tue/Thu -Sun 8pm–10pm, Sat–Sun 10am–1pm (Aug–Mar), www.eissporthalle-benrath.de*
- ***Düsseltal,*** *Eisstadion an der Brehmstraße, Brehmstr. 27, Tel. (02 11) 8 99 53 20, Mon–Fri 4pm–6pm and Mon/Fri 8pm–10pm, Sat/Sun11am–1pm, 2pm–4pm and 5pm–7pm (Aug–Mar)*

Running

Düsseldorf has lots of scenic running routes to offer. Challenge yourself on trails in Grafenberger and Aaper Wald, run around Unterbacher See, enjoy the beauty of Benrather Schlosspark or meet many other runners jogging along the Rhine. If you want to combine a nice run with an entertaining guided tour along the highlights of the city or nature resorts, book a unique sightrunning event.

- *Run & See Düsseldorf, Tel. (02 11) 6 58 59 25, www.run-and-see-duesseldorf.de*
- *Sportamt, Arena-Straße. 1, Tel. (02 11) 8 99 52 03, www.duesseldorf.de/sportamt*

Swimming

No lack of swimming pools, you can choose from eleven pools. Attractive: leisure pool Düsselstrand (fun for the whole family) or the Rhine

ESPRIT-Arena

SPORTS CENTRES

Arena-Sportpark

Round the ESPRIT-Arena you'll find numerous sports facilities: several artificial grass fields, in-line skating, hockey and basketball fields. Athletes can practise outside on the track or inside the modern athletic sports hall.

■ ***Stockum,*** *Arena-Str. 1, Tel. (02 11) 8 99 52 30, Mon–Fri 7am–9.30pm, Sat 7am–6pm, Sun 7am–5pm, Nov 1.–Mar 31. Sun 7am–4pm*

Burg-Wächter Castello

The basketball players of Magics and the handball players of HSG were more than pleased when they got their new home in the South of Düsseldorf worth 28 million Euros. The multi purpose-hall Burg-Wächter Castello is used as gym by schools and is an ideal location for clubs with its 3,400 seats for spectators.

■ ***Reisholz,*** *Karl-Hohmann-Str. 1 HSG, Tel. (0 18 05) 63 33 37, www.hsg-duesseldorf.de; Magics, Tel. (02 11) 90 48 55 81, www.duesseldorfmagics.com*

ISS Dome

ISS Dome is the last in the series of new sports centres in Düsseldorf: finished in September 2006. The multi-purpose hall offers seats for 13,400 spectators when ice hockey is played. There are 1,900 parking spaces, and a shuttle bus service between S-stations Rath and Unterrath. Main user is DEG Metro Stars in the German ice hockey league (DEL).

■ ***Rath,*** *Theodorstr. 281, Tel. (02 11) 8 92 77 00, tickets Tel. (02 11) 77 50 57, www.iss-dome.de*

ESPRIT-Arena

The stadium offers luxury: 51,500 spectators have covered seats: the roof is convertible and heaters guarantee weather independence. 22,000 parking spaces and train connection via U 78 avoid traffic jams at the beginning or end, for example, at football matches by Fortuna.

■ ***Stockum,*** *Arena-Str. 1, Tel. (02 11) 15 98 12 00, www.espritarena.de*

pool in Stockum (perfect for practising, with outdoor pool). There are not many swimming clubs: well known is the club Freie Schwimmer.

- ***Flingern,*** *Freie Schwimmer, Flinger Broich 91, Tel. (02 11) 23 19 10, www.freie-schwimmer.de*
- ***Flingern,*** *Freizeitbad Düsselstrand, Kettwiger Str. 50, Tel. (02 11) 8 21 62 20, Mon–Fri 6.30am–11pm (sports pool), Mon–Fri 10am–11pm, Sat/Sun 9am–8pm (the whole pool)*
- ***Niederkassel,*** *DLRG Bezirk Düsseldorf, Niederkasseler Deich 293, Tel. (02 11) 59 13 13, www.dlrg.de*
- ***Stockum,*** *Rheinbad, Europaplatz 1, Tel. (02 11) 8 21 29 83, Mon–Fri 6am–9pm, Sat/Sun 8am–8pm, www.baeder-dusseldorf.de*

Sailing

Unterbacher See and the Rhine offer ideal conditions for sailing. The yacht club on the Rhine offers training courses for children and you can rent a berth. Club Unterbacher See is more easygoing: have fun while sailing. Children can learn on club-owned boats.

- ***Golzheim,*** *Düsseldorfer Yachtclub, Rotterdamer Str. 30, Tel. (02 11) 43 28 02, www.dyc.de*
- ***Unterbach,*** *Segel-Kameradschaft Unterbacher See, Tel. (02 11), 7 40 43 82, www.sku-duesseldorf.de*

GETTING AROUND

Blauer See

The "blue lake" is 2 hectares in size and was formerly a quarry. Steep banks show the change from limestone into dolomite. Visitors can explore the rock face – a nature reserve – with hired boats. A wide range of leisure activities (for a fee): fairytale zoo, crazy golf, pony track, an open air theater and much more.

- ***Ratingen,*** *Zum Blauen See 20, Tel. (0 21 02) 55 64 32, www.blauersee-ratingen.de*

Boat tours

The shipping line Köln-Düsseldorfer offers daily trips in and around Düsseldorf: a one-hour tour on the Rhine to explore the city, medieval Zons or the biggest European river port in Duisburg. Enjoy the beautiful panorama and have a cup of coffee with a piece of cake or pasta or paella with live music.

Boat tour on the Rhine

LEISURE PARKS

The municipal leisure park **Heerdt** offers leisure activities for every age group: a playground for small children, climbing frames, fields for handball, volley ball or badminton, billiards, bowls, crazy golf and a skater track. In a multi-purpose hall you can rent games and playing equipment.

Gutshof Niederheid is the centre of the leisure park **Niederheider Wäldchen** (230,000 square metres). The historical farmstead from the 13th century is a children's farm and a riding stable today. The city of Düsseldorf bought the place in 1973 to save the green belt for recreation and leisure. Very attractive: children's birthday parties on the farm. The leisure centre **Ulenbergstraße** offers playgrounds for small and older children. Visitors can choose between different ball games, crazy golf, bowls and trampoline. In a hall you can play table tennis or table football. Keep-fit apparatus and playing equipment are available free of charge.

- ***Flehe,*** *Ulenbergstr. 11, Tel. (02 11) 15 25 20 or 8 99 48 00, Mar–Sep daily from 9am, Oct–Feb daily from 10am*
- ***Heerdt,*** *Heerdter Landstr. 160, Tel. (02 11) 5 04 79 70, Apr–Sep Tue-Sun 11am-8pm, Oct-Mai Tue-Sun 11am-9pm*
- ***Holthausen,*** *Bonner Str. 121, Tel. (02 11) 7 90 03 94 or (01 71) 2 19 02 33, Tue-Sun 2pm–7pm, Bauernhof Tue–Sun from 2pm, www.gut-niederheid.de*
- ***Köln-Düsseldorfer,*** *Tel. (02 11) 3 23 92 63, Easter–October quay Altstadt/ Burgplatz, www.k-d.com*

Cycle tours

If you plan a tour along the Rhine by tandem or with a wheelchair user you'll get all the information you need at the information centre of the Allgemeine Deutsche Fahrrad-Club Düsseldorf (association of cycle clubs). They lend bicycles (even with stabilizers), provide maps and brochures for tours and tell you how to look after your bike.

- ***Oberbilk,*** *Siemensstr. 46, Tel. (02 11) 99 22 55, www.adfc-duesseldorf.de*

Düsseldorf by bike

In Düsseldorf, cyclists are in the lucky position to be able to see almost all the attractions in the city centre without getting off their saddle. At specially interesting points, the guide stops to inform the participants about the city history and tourist highlights.
Duration 2 hours, for groups from 10 persons onwards incl. bike rental and guide

- *Contact Düsseldorf Marketing & Tourismus GmbH Tel. (0211) 17 202 -854 www.visitduesseldorf.de*

Grüner See

At the edge of Düsseldorf is the large recreation park Volkardey (110 hectares). On summer days there are up to 25,000 nature fans on their way. The "green lake" is part of the park, swimming is not allowed, but in certain areas surfing and boating are permitted. There are many small barbecue sites and even a barbecue hut.

- ***Ratingen,*** *Volkardeyer Str., Tel. (0 21 02) 5 50 52 22, www.ratingen.de*

Guided City Tours

Skilled and entertaining tour guides offer a variety of guided walks throughout the city. There are many topics to chose from, ranging from Altstadt- and Media harbor tours over walks through Kaiserswerth, Altbier-tastings, and scary night-walks down to art explorations.

- *Contact Düsseldorf Marketing & Tourismus GmbH Tel. (0211) 17 20217 202-854, www.visitduesseldorf.de/en/tours*
- *Contact Düsseldorfer Stadtführer e. V., Tel (01 77) 4 28 35 48 www.duesseldorfer-stadtfuehrer.de*
- *Contact Altbier Agentur Eberhard Fischer e. K., Tel (01 72) 7 06 15 07, www.altbier-safari.de*

Guided Nature Tours

The Düsseldorfer Gartenamt (garden administration) is prepared for fans of gardens, parks and landscape and nature reserves. There are about 75 guided tours on offer. The popular tours include nature reserves, historical parks, forests and cemeteries. And you can get to know Hofgarten and Nordpark.

DÜSSELDORF PARKS

Hofgarten

The oldest park in Düsseldorf, Hofgarten, is an oasis in the city: relaxation on the lawns (entrance Ehrenhof and Inselstr.), playgrounds for the little ones (entrance Kaiserstr.) and art along the way. Garden architect Maximilian Weyhe created a wide landscape with gentle slopes and a large pond using astonishingly little space.

Nordpark, Japanischer Garten

Beautifully designed flower beds and an interesting water garden are the highlights of the park. A jewel in the crown is the Japanese garden made by a garden artist from the Far East. Aquazoo, the exhibition centre "Ballhaus" and a café are part of the Nordpark. (Entrance Kaiserswerther Str. 390.)

Volksgarten, Südpark, Botanischer Garten

A line of green parks goes all the way from Oberbilk via Wersten to the Rhine. It starts with the Volksgarten, a landscaped park with pond. Südpark follows; it was established for the federal garden exhibition in 1987. The park has gardens with special themes, a small lake landscaped, a pets' corner, a water playground and a garden restaurant. The south entrance leads to with the botanical garden of the university.

Drachenbootregatta on the Rhine

■ *Contact Gartenamt, Kaiserswerther Str. 390, Tel. (02 11) 8 99 48 00, www.duesseldorf.de*

Schloss Heltorf

Castle Heltorf has belonged to the Dukes of Spee since 1662. The forestry commission with the Spee's coat-of-arms is now in its 12th generation. Farming and forestry have been going on for more than 900 years. The castle is privately owned and cannot be visited. The park is worth a visit.

■ ***Angermund,** Am Froschenteich (at the B 8), Tel. (02 03) 74 64 65, May–Oct Sat/Sun/public holidays 10am–6pm, www.forst-graf-spee.de*

Unterbacher See

An artificial lake of 87 hectares and up to 13,4 metres deep; you can go sailing, canoeing, rowing and fishing.

■ ***Unterbach,** Kleiner Torfbruch 31, Tel. (02 11) 8 99 20 94, beach pools May–Sep Mon/Tue/Thu 10am–8pm, Wed/Fri/Sat 10am–9pm, Sun 9am–8pm, Boats Apr–Oct Mon–Fri 1pm–8pm, Sat/Sun 11am–8pm, www.unterbachersee.com*

EVENTS

Bücherbummel

For four days once a year Kö transforms into a huge open air bookshop. Antiquarian booksellers, regional bookshops, publishing companies, literary institutes and municipal institutes present themselves on more than 130 stalls and on different stages. You are invited to look around, to listen, to watch and to buy.

■ ***Stadtmitte,** Königsallee, Tel. (02 11) 57 59 50, Jun, www.buecherbummel-auf-der-koe.de*

Büchermeile

For a whole weekend, you can browse through books. The promenade on the Rhine extends from Burgplatz to Alter Hafen: a huge choice of old and new books along the book mile and a programme to go with it: you get information on bookbinding and paper art.

▪ ***Altstadt,*** *Rheinuferpromenade contact: Altstadt Marketing, Tel. (02 11) 32 95 94, May/Jun/Sep*

Carnival

When women in fancy dress attack the city hall and cut men's ties, then it is Altweiberfastnacht (Thursday preceding Ash Wednesday). You love it or you hate it. You can't understand why people enjoy dancing and drinking in packed pubs and streets for three days. The highlight of the three crazy days is the carnival parade on Monday before Ash Wednesday, called "Rosenmontagszug" or "Zoch". Thousands of people watch and greet the carnival princes with "Helau".

▪ ***Centre,*** *contact: Comittee Düsseldorfer Carneval e.V., Zollstr. 9, Tel. (02 11) 33 01 01, Feb, www.comitee-duesseldorfer-carneval.de*

Christmas Market

Starting at the end of November more than 200 stalls decorated in Christmas-style with thousands of lights offer seasonal bits and bobs: Christmas decorations, knitwear and wood carvings.

▪ ***Stadtmitte,*** *end of Nov–Dec 23rd, Sun–Thu 11am–8pm, Fri/Sat 11am–9pm, www.duesseldorf-tourismus.de*

Drachenbootregatta

Teams of firms, social institutes, schools, clubs, and groups of friends paddle to win the much-loved Drachenpokal (dragon trophy). Anybody can take part, you have to subscribe beforehand – a professional cox and equipment are provided. The regatta is a merry and convivial event. Be part of the crowd.

▪ ***Hafen,*** *contact: Stadtwerke Düsseldorf AG, Tel. (08 00) 3 03 28 08, Jul, www.drachenbootregatta.de*

Düsseldorf Festival

In 1991 a private initiative founded the cultural festival Altstadtherbst (now called Düsseldorf Festival) which has reached regional importance. About 20,000 visitors join 60 events in two weeks and get well entertained: opera in industrial plants, unconventional and exceptional performances from all over the world.

▪ ***Altstadt,*** *contact: Düsseldorf Festival GmbH, Bolkerstr. 14-16, Tel. (02 11) 8 28 26 60, Sep, www.duesseldorf-festival.de*

Frankreich-Festival

To honour France Düsseldorf celebrates July 14th (French national holiday) every year. The old part of the town becomes "Petit Paris". The festival aims to celebrate the diverse cultural, economical and friendly connections between the two countries.

▪ ***Altstadt,*** *contact: Destination Düsseldorf e. V., Tel. (02 11) 45 60-539, Jul, www.duesseldorfer-frankreich-fest.de*

Fun Fair

Every year, in the third week of July more than 300 brand new and traditional fun fair rides attract millions of people. An important highlight of the fun fair week is the huge fireworks.

- ***Oberkasseler Rheinwiese,*** *contact: Düsseldorf Marketing & Tourismus GmbH, Tel. (02 11) 1 72 02 14, Jul, www.duesseldorf-tourismus.de*

Japantag

About 7,000 Japanese people live in Düsseldorf. That's why the city is called Klein Tokio. Every year the Japanese community organises a Japan day together with the city of Düsseldorf and the state NRW: an extensive cultural and entertainment programme attracts visitors. A final top event is the huge fireworks.

- ***Oberkasseler Rheinwiesen,*** *contact: Düsseldorf Marketing & Tourismus GmbH, Tel. (02 11) 1 72 02 28, Jun, www.duesseldorf-tourismus.de, www.japantag-duesseldorf.de*

Jazz-Rally

Every year, on the last weekend in June: jazz-rally in Düsseldorf. It is known for its wide musical range and top-class performances: merry Dixieland and swing, rock, blues, fusion, tango, bossa nova, motown, funk and much more.

- ***Centre,*** *contact: Destination Düsseldorf, Tel. (02 11) 45 60-539, Jun, www.duesseldorfer-jazzrally.de*

Mittsommernacht

In June, during the longest day of the year, you can sit down at a table on the Rhine promenade and enjoy Midsummer's Night. After sunset you can watch the fireworks from there.

- ***Altstadt,*** *contact: Düsseldorf Marketing & Tourismus GmbH, Tel. (02 11) 17 20 20, Jun, www.duesseldorf-tourismus.de*

It's Japantag

Jazz -Rally

Nacht der Museen

A late night visit to a museum has a special attraction for those who don't go that often during the day. The institutes discovered this marketing chance and offer one ticket valid for all museums on a special night. There are open-air venues throughout the night.

- ***Downtown,*** *April, www.nacht-der-museen.de/duesseldorf*

Radschläger-Turnier

Every year, boys and girls follow an old tradition and present cartwheels along the Rhine water front. Those who show the best and fastest presentation will get a prize. Children from eight to twelve can participate.

- ***Stadtmitte,*** *contact: Alde Düsseldorfer-Bürgergesellschaft von 1920 e.V., Tel. (02 11) 9 72 17 10, Jun, www.alde-duesseldorfer.de*

Rheinmarathon

In 2003 the Rhine marathon, also called MetroGroupMarathon Düsseldorf started for the first time. It goes along a very attractive route leading along Königsallee, troughout the city, over one of the Rhine bridges and finishing on the Rhine promenade. The spectators are fantastic and the supporting programme is fun.

- ***Downtown,*** *contact: rheinmarathon düsseldorf e.V., Tel. (02 11) 6 10 19 00, May, www.metrogroup-marathon.de*

Cartwheeler

Schumannfestival

The Robert-Schumann-Association Düsseldorf organizes a Schumann festival every two years in May. Schumann was municipal musical director during his last active years in Düsseldorf. For two weeks the city commemorates the great musician in several concerts in different concert halls.

■ ***Downtown,*** *contact: Festivalbüro, Tel. (02 11) 13 32 22, May/Jun, www.schumannfest-duesseldorf.de*

Stadtwerke Düsseldorf Kö-Lauf

The city's department of works invites everybody to their Kö-run on the last Sunday in September: little ones with their parents, amateur runners, German top runners.

■ ***Stadtmitte,*** *contact: Stadtwerke Düsseldorf AG, Tel. (02 11) 61 01 90, Sep, www.swd-koelauf.de*

WELLNESS

Hamam Sahara Wellness

It feels like being in Turkey: Hamam Sahara Wellness centre is a stone's throw from the main station. Following the Oriental washing rites Amal M'Charrak and his team work their clients' skins. Massage of the back or the whole body with aroma oil (Royal) cost extra.

■ ***Friedrichstadt,*** *Mintropstr. 21, Tel. (02 11) 2 71 33 21, ladies Mon/Tue/Thu/Fri 12pm–11pm, Sun 10am–11pm, men Wed/Sat 12pm–11pm, www.hamamsahara.de*

Münster-Therme

The old swimming pool in Münsterstraße was renovated and is now Münster-Therme with classical ambience in art deco and from the 1870s. An outdoor pool (water at 32 degrees), a thermal spa, two saunas and a steam bath belong to the wellness centre. A real event: the moonshine sauna with live music and buffet, three times a year.

■ ***Pempelfort,*** *Münsterstr. 13, Tel. (02 11) 8 21 26 32, Tue/Thu 6.30am-9pm, Wed/Fri 6.30-10pm, Sat/Sun 8am-5pm, Sat/Sun/public holidays 8am–5pm, ladies Wed, www.baeder-duesseldorf.de*

Münster-Therme with classical ambience

Neandertal-Therme

Hotel Gut Höhne has one of the nicest sauna parks in the surroundings of Düsseldorf, near Hubbelrath. The pool has 30 degrees water temperature and the hot pool even 35 degrees.

■ ***Mettmann,*** *Düsseldorfer Str. 253, Tel. (0 21 04) 77 80, www.guthoehne.de*

Sauna Benrath

Düsseldorf's second thermal spa lies in the south district of Benrath. It was opened in 2006: 100 cubic metres of salt water for 80 square metres; 32 degrees water temperature and all sorts of fancy showers that massage your neck or your back and make your skin tingle. A sauna park completes the wellness centre.

■ ***Benrath,*** *Regerstr. 5, Tel. (02 11) 8 21 94 31, Tue–Fri 10am–9pm, Sat/Sun/public holidays 8am–7pm, www.baeder-duesseldorf.de*

Spa-Club Nikko

Relaxing on the 11th floor; the Japanese hotel Nikko has had a new wellness centre since 2006. 550 square metres with saunas, Sanarium (mild sauna with aroma oil) and beauty and massage treatment. The spa-club is open to non-residents.

■ ***Stadtmitte,*** *Immermannstr. 41, Tel. (02 11) 8 34 25 00, Mo 11am–22pm, Tue–Sat 7am–10pm, Sun 8am-10pm, www.nikko-hotel.de*

ENLAND
gummi-Paradies
WMF
tatzino
Snac

Snackkarte
Capri
Panini

TIPS

Whether you want to have a quick meal after a long day of sightseeing or want to spend a wonderful evening with an excellent dinner - the manifold offers of Düsseldorf's gastronomic scene will leave nothing to be desired. For everyone's taste and budget you'll find the right place. Those who like home-style cooking as well as those who prefer a more exotic or fancy cuisine will be completely satisfied.

The following categories will help you to make the right choice: **Quick meals** - here you can have a good and convenient meal, or even just a snack. **Breweries** - they represent the solid and orig-inal side of Düsseldorf. Good to know: your empty beer glass will be automatically refilled unless you tell them to stop. **Good value** - here you'll find the right place if you just want to enjoy a tasty meal after a long exhaustive shopping tour. **Moderate and good** - in these restaurants you'll get delicious meals at reasonable prices. **For gourmets** - sometimes you need to treat yourself to culinary delights. Reservation recommended. **Pure luxury** - enjoy a special evening and take your time to wine and dine. Please book in advance. **Cafes** - enticing sweets and hearty snacks invite you to take more. **Bars and pubs** - yummy cocktails will make your day. Clubs - After a good dinner enjoy yourself on the dance floor.

Uerige
The brewery serves at bar tables outside even at sub zero temperatures and its pea soup attracts all Düsseldorf on Saturdays at 11am.
➲**page 57**

Reusch
Reusch is known as a place for mussels but it also offers tasty and traditional food. ➲**page 61**

Kikaku
It's probably the best and the most typical Sushi restaurant in town with a wide choice of bite-size portions. ➲**page 65**

Münstermanns Kontor
The kitchen is known for carefully selected ingredients; typical European food is served in the ambience of a French bistro.
➲**page 66**

Robert's Bistro
Experts on French food enjoy fish soup, oysters or tongue of veal with foie gras. ➲**page 66**

Berens am Kai
Scarcely a chef is as creative as Holger Berens. His fine cuisine enjoys an excellent reputation.
➲**page69**

Heinemann
Heinemann's sweets and cakes are famous all over the world. Even Pope Benedict loves the gateaux and flans of this very popular pastry shop. ➲**page 71**

REALLY COSY: BREWERIES

In the old days they were all over the place, these small pubs where during the night beer was brewed and guests drank it during the day. Four of these home breweries made it into our millennium. Be it **Füchschen, Uerige, Schlüssel** or **Schumacher,** each has its own die-hard fans. They would never allow a drop of any other Alt to run down their throats. This is not only true for locals but also for tourists (it goes without saying that you shouldn't miss this charming part of Düsseldorf). A true local sticks to "his/her" Alt a life time.

While the nation-wide consumption of Alt has gone down, its popularity in Düsseldorf has steadily been rising. Not only did this cause a new start-up brewery to try its luck, but the people's growing concern for health also made way for mixed drinks. They combine non-alcoholic beer with lemonade (Fassbrause), for example.

Some information on a **Köbes** (which is what waiters in Düsseldorf's breweries are called): They are very similar to the beer and the menu –hearty, simple, good and rather down to earth. If you don't know them you might be irritated: cheeky and outspoken they are always ready for a joke. Order some water and you might be asked "Would you like soap and a towel?" Order a Haxe (pork leg), a must on the scrubbed wooden tables, he will serve it as "a diet". These days their comments are friendly and humorous. In the old days they could be quite offensive, even aggressive especially when a guest ordered a Kölsch (beer from Cologne) in a Düsseldorf brewery. Harshness is bad for business and so the Köbesse were trained to be witty and original. There are a few female Köbesse but they are still an absolute exception.

Due to the tourists Düsseldorf Platt (Low German) is no longer obligatory in the breweries. **Füchschen's Haxen** (pork legs), **Schumacher's Sauerbraten** (beef prepared with apple treacle), **Uerige's Rosenkränzchen** (rings of grilled sausages with cole slaw), **Flöns** (a sort of black pudding) and **Ölk** (onions) are no longer a secret to the tourist. **Halve Hahn** (Mainzer cheese made of sour milk with caraway seed on rye rolls), and **Mettbrötchen** (rolls with spicy minced meat), that's what you find in every brewery. By the way, a Köbes once declared Mettbrötchen as "German sushi" to a Japanese tourist – an explanation that is still going strong.

Düsseldorf: Hospitality at its best

★ **Uerige** is a curiosity at any time of the day.

▮ ***Altstadt,*** *Berger Str. 1, Tel. (02 11) 86 69 90, daily 10am–12am, cash only*

Im Füchschen, the owner is not only called König (king) - he was once a carnival prince.

▮ ***Altstadt,*** *Ratinger Str. 28, Tel. (02 11) 1 37 47 16, Mon–Thu 9am–1am, Fri/Sat 9am–2am, Sun 9am–12am*

Schlösser Quartier Bohème, with its elegant bar and lounge, is equally attractive to young people and traditional associations.

▮ ***Altstadt,*** *Ratinger Str. 25, Tel. (02 11) 15 97 61 50, Sun–Thu 11am–12am, Fri/Sat 11am–3am*

Schumacher has two breweries. Next to classics like sour kidneys with creamy mashed potatoes you'll even get light vegetarian meals on the menu.

▮ ***Altstadt,*** *Im Goldenen Kessel, Bolkerstr. 44, Tel. (02 11) 32 60 07, Sun–Thu 10am–12am, Fri/Sat 10am–1am*

▮ ***Stadtmitte,*** *Oststr. 123, Tel. (02 11) 32 60 04, Sun–Thu 10am–12am, Fri/Sat 10am–1am*

Frankenheim is not right in the centre and relies more on its regulars than tourists. Here you can get Rhineland specialities but also chicken wings and tortilla chips – to suit all ages.

▮ ***Pempelfort,*** *Wielandstr. 12, Tel. (02 11) 35 14 47, Mon-Sat 10am–1am, Sun 10am-12pm*

Kürzer is Düsseldorf's latest "old beer" and was created in 2010.

▮ ***Altstadt,*** *Kurze Str. 18–20, Tel. (02 11) 32 26 96 , daily 11am–3am*

Zum Goldenen Ring is said to have existed since the 16th century. Newly decorated, the house presents itself as a good mixture of tradition and modernism.

▮ ***Altstadt,*** *Burgplatz 21, Tel. (02 11) 87 55 03 33, Sun–Thu 10.30am–12pm, Fri/Sat 10.30am–1pm*

Zum Schlüssel is the name of the brewery and the beer, which is still being brewed there.
Guided tours for groups.

▮ ***Altstadt,*** *Bolkerstr. 41–47, Tel. (02 11) 8 28 95 50, Sun-Thu 10am-12pm, Fri/Sat 10am-1am*

QUICK MEALS

Ab der Fisch

This pub is a real institution in Derendorf and Pempelfort. It is always packed. The menu offers traditional pub food with a Mediterranean touch, salads and pasta. Breakfast till 3pm.

▮ ***Pempelfort,*** *Moltkestr. 124, Tel. (02 11) 48 25 88, Mon–Thu 9am–1am, Fri/Sat 9am–2am, cash only Sun 9am-12pm*

Beethoven

Chopin would be more suitable for this pub with its charming interior and its cosy small beer garden. The menu is tasty and on the light side. But as it is in Beethovenstraße, a bust of the deaf musician occupies a central position.

▮ ***Flingern,*** *Ackerstr. 106, Tel. (02 11) 6 79 09 73, Mon–Sat 10am–1am, Sun 10am–12am, cash only*

Berliner Imbiss

The home of the Currywurst (fried sausages with curry sauce) is Berlin but after the first ones were sold from a stand in Kaiserswerth, the spicy originals can be bought at various places. The spiciest in town is called "Berliner knock out".

▮ ***Kaiserswerth,*** *Klemensplatz, daily 10.30am–10pm*

Bistro Zicke

Movie-time deco, this pub is the home of students, young mothers and business men. The interior is slightly shabby which adds to its charm: bistro food from Bavarian to Mediterranean.

▮ ***Carlstadt,*** *Bäckerstr. 5a, Tel. (02 11) 32 40 56, daily 9am–1am, cash only*

Böser Chinese

Modern Chinese cuisine in stylish ambience. Generous servings and fresh as can be. Hafen, Zollhof 13,

▮ ***Hafen,*** *Zollhof 13, Tel. (02 11) 30 33 78 87, Mon-Fri 12am-3pm and 5.30pm -12pm, Sat/Sun 12am-12pm*

Buttershaker

Chicken wings, spare ribs and burgers, Texas steaks and Mexican nachos are on the menu. A huge TV is for sports fans, very American. The kitchen is open till 1am.

▮ ***Stadtmitte,*** *Worringer Str. 142, Tel. (02 11) 3 69 41 88, Sun–Thu 11am–1am, Fri/Sat 11am–2am*

Café Florian

With old metal signs, art deco lamps and benches covered in red velvet, this regionally well-known café has a touch of belle époque: traditional food; breakfast till 5pm for those who sleep in.

▮ ***Pempelfort,*** *Nordstr. 56, Tel. (02 11) 49 89 80, daily 9am–1am, cash only*

Cubar

Central American flair: breakfast and lunchtime buffet with traditional and modern Cuban food. In the evening: an event buffet, vegetables, fish, seafood, meat or poultry, everything is prepared in front of you.

Curry

- ***Derendorf,*** *Rather Str. 110a, Tel. (02 11) 6 01 04 70, Mon–Thu 9am–1am, Fri/Sat 9am–open end, Sun 10am–1am*

Curry
Very typically Düsseldorf: posh stands at two places, curry fried sausages and French fries with aioli or other sauces even with gold leaves; for quick meals; friendly.

- ***Unterbilk,*** *Hammer Str. 2, Tel. (02 11) 3 03 28 57, Sun–Thu 11.30am–11pm, Fri/Sat 11.30am–12am, cash only*
- ***Pempelfort,*** *Moltkestr. 115, Tel. (02 11) 5 14 32 56, Sun–Thu 11.30am–11pm, Fri/Sat 11.30am–11pm, cash only*

Curry Stars
No fried sausage will be like this one. Curry Stars specializes in the most delicious fried sausages. Try his home-made potato chips, they are worth sinning for. Lamb fillet and a wide variety of sauces: sweet, fruity, spicy or with pepper.

- ***Oberkassel,*** *Oberkasseler Str. 73/ Entrance Luegallee, Tel. (02 11) 9 55 96 39, Mon–Fr 10am–3.30pm, cash only*

Die Geissel
A huge board informs you of the daily changing and very creative menu. Creativity is everywhere: discount coupons when it is raining, a flexible party service, affordable lunches and W-Lan broadband for workaholics.

- ***Bilk,*** *Aachener Str. 58, Tel. (02 11) 6 00 28 89 11, Sun-Thu 11am–12pm, Fri/Sat 11am–1am, cash only*

Hot la Cucina
It is the smallest trattoria in Oberkassel and it is always packed. Waiting is worthwhile, delicious pasta and thin pizzas are of high quality.

- ***Oberkassel,*** *Dominikanerstr. 14, Tel. (02 11) 55 64 18, Mon–Fri 12pm–2.30pm and 6pm–10.30pm, Sat/Sun 6pm–10.30pm, cash only*

Julian's
Bar and restaurant of the Courtyard Mariott offer a surprising mixture of food like the Caribbean coco-mango soup; in summer you can enjoy your cocktail on the terrace with a spectacular view of the harbour.

- ***Hafen,*** *in Courtyard by Marriot Hotel, Speditionstr. 11, Tel. (02 11) 49 39 20 07, daily 12pm–12am*

Klee's
A mixture of bar, pub and restaurant in the art collection K20 building. It was a lounge long before the term became known. It meets the expectations of pampered dinner guests and coffee-drinking tourists; high quality.

▪ ***Altstadt,*** *Grabbeplatz 5, Tel. (02 11) 16 84 48 16, Tue–Thu 10am–12am,Fri/Sat 10am-1am, Sun 10am-10pm*

Löffelbar

The name is misleading: soup as well as sandwiches, salads and a daily menu. Nevertheless, soups prevail; according to your appetite you choose cup A, B or C and according to your taste from traditional to Asian.

▪ ***Pempelfort,*** *Tußmannstr. 3, Tel. (02 11) 4 40 32 78, Mo-Fr 10am–late, Sat/Sun 9am-late, cash only*

Loft

Enjoy a fresh and healthy meal in a vintage style bistro. Order at the counter and it will be ready within minutes. You can tell by the taste that the curries and the ice-cream is home-made.

▪ ***Hafen,*** *Hammer Str. 4, Tel. (0211)15 92 05 40, Mon-Fri 11am-10pm, Sat/Sun 10am-10pm*

Marktwirtschaft

This pub has been the meeting point of artists, critics, media people and stall holders for twenty years. Directly on Carlsplatz it serves the earliest breakfast in town (from 7am).

▪ ***Carlstadt,*** *Benrather Str. 7, Tel. (02 11) 8 60 68 48, Mon–Thu 8am–12am, Fr 8am–1am, Sat 7am–1am (food till 11pm), Sun 10am–6pm (Sep–May), cash only*

Muggel

Locals of Oberkassel call it the sitting room; it is a real must; cinema in the basement for movie fans and the café-restaurant for the jet-set; specialities Düsseldorf-style and Mediterranean food.

▪ ***Oberkassel,*** *Dominikanerstr. 4, Tel. (02 11) 55 41 82, Mon–Thu 8.30am–1am, Fr 8.30am–2am, Sat 9am–2am, Sun 9.30am–1am (food till 11pm)*

Ohme Jupp

At Ratinger Straße, this pub is exceptional: in the mornings coffee with milk and breakfast buffet, at lunchtime, business people have traditional lunches and in the evening: party for everyone.

▪ ***Altstadt,*** *Ratinger Str. 19, Tel. (02 11) 32 64 06, Mon–Sat 8am–1am, Sun 10am–1am (food daily til 11pm), cash only*

Qüche

It is a safe bet to eat where landlords and restaurant owners eat. A small soup restaurant with tasty and healthy food; waiters eat there to relax from the stressful work of serving at the longest beer bar of the world. Three times a week night owls are catered for.

Ohme Jupp

■ ***Altstadt,*** *Kurze Str. 3, Tel. (02 11) 8 36 90 58, Mon–Fri 12pm–4pm and Wed/Fri/ Sat 7pm–1am, cash only*

Reusch

Reusch is known as a place for mussels but the kitchen also offers tasty and rustic food. The mussels are delicious: classic Rhineland-style, fried or with melted cheese on top.

■ ***Unterbilk,*** *Erftstr. 20, Tel. (02 11) 39 10 33, Mon–Fri 12pm–2.30pm and daily from 6pm*

Sassafras

A traditional pub in Oberkassel; food is always good, huge salads and the pasta really fill you up. It is famous for its carnival parties. That's where it's all happening.

■ ***Oberkassel,*** *Düsseldorfer Str. 90, Tel. (02 11) 55 10 75, Mon–Thu 5pm–1am, Fri/Sat 5pm–3am, Sun 4pm–12am, cash only*

SchnellVeg

Full-fledged vegetarian-vegan cuisine in a non-chalant interior. Fast food goes vegan: Burgers and pizzas are come in various combinations. Choose between three different types of meat-substitutes on your home-made bun and order fresh sides to your delight.

■ ***Pempelfort,*** *Bagelstr. 130, Tel. (02 11) 91 18 47 28, Tue-Sun 10am-1am*

Schwan

Landlady Kerstin Schwan (swan) owns three "swans", one in Derendorf, one in the old part of the city and one in Pempelfort. They all have an excellent breakfast menu and offer European-Asian food.

■ ***Altstadt,*** *Mühlenstr. 2, Tel. (02 11) 1 36 53 87, Sun–Thur 10am–12am, Fr/Sat 10am–1am*

■ ***Derendorf,*** *Frankenstraße 1, Tel. (02 11) 39 31 13, Mon–Sun 10am–12am*

■ ***Pempelfort,*** *Sternstraße 50, Tel. (02 11) 49 76 99 59, Mon–Thu 8.30am-12pm, Fri/Sat 8.30am-12pm, Sun 9.30am-11pm*

Ugly Deluxe

It's just not true; there is nothing ugly in this bar. The combination of bar, lounge and restaurant with chandeliers is stylish and luxurious. Indian soup, Italian pasta, French pies and Spanish tapas are on offer.

■ ***Bilk,*** *Karolinger Str. 80, Tel. (02 11) 3 11 93 54, Mon-Sat 10am-1am, Sun 10am-6pm, cash only*

Vapiano

Vapiano proves quick meals can be healthy and tasty. You can watch how pasta and pizza are prepared and salads made.

■ ***Stadtmitte,*** *Martin-Luther-Platz 28, Tel. (02 11) 6 17 33 66, Mon–Thur 10am–12am, Fr/Sat 10am–1am, Sun 12pm–11pm*

■ ***Derendorf,*** *Kaiserswerther Str. 229, Tel. (02 11) 98 48 78 66, Mon–Thu 10am–12am, Fri/Sat 10am–1am, Sun 12pm–11pm*

Zum Hirschchen

Belongs to the Schlösser brewery which is part of the Dr. Oetker Company. Alt is served the American way in 1.5 litre jugs. Food is regional and typical.

▪ ***Pempelfort,*** *Alt-Pempelfort 2, Tel. (02 11) 1 71 14 05, Mon–Thu 11.30am–12pm, Fri/Sat 11.30am–1am, Sun 10am–11pm (food 11am–10.30pm)*

GOOD VALUE

Am Zault

The inn is 200 years old. Elegantly decorated, a quick and friendly service. A bar with 50 tasty tapas. Insider tip for night owls: the chef invites you to a midnight soup.

▪ ***Unterbach,*** *Gerresheimer Landstr. 40, Tel. (02 11) 25 10 81, daily 12pm–2pm and 6pm–10pm*

Carissima

Without question, the best lasagne in town: a journey to Carissima is worthwhile. This typical Italian trattoria is always packed; try their speciality taglierini with Porcini mushrooms; large portions.

Casa Luigi

▪ ***Oberkassel,*** *Luegallee 17, Tel. (02 11) 57 14 51, daily 12pm–11.30pm*

Casa Luigi

Luigi allows an open view of the kitchen. He offers first-class Italian food professionally prepared and served; always friendly even under stress.

▪ ***Carlstadt,*** *Hohe Str. 33, Tel. (02 11) 32 73 01, Mon–Sat 12pm–11pm*

Die Ente

You won't believe it but you do get geese, a speciality between November 10th and Christmas. Apart from that you'll get what the name promises: a wide range of duck. And the decorations are full of ducks, too.

▪ ***Unterbach,*** *Rathelbeckstr. 319, Tel. (02 11) 20 27 48, Tue–Sun 5.30pm–12am*

Durians

The most authentic Thai food in Düsseldorf; the ten tables in a former ice café are always packed. A must is Tom Kha Gai, a traditional, slightly spicy Thai chicken soup with coconut and ginger.

▪ ***Oberkassel,*** *Sonderburgstr. 25, Tel. (02 11) 9 54 27 79, Tue–Sun 6pm–11pm, cash only*

Himmel & Ähd

Tradition meets trend: concrete ceilings and life-size pheasants on the walls. Düsseldorf mustard roast, Himmel and Ähd (sky and earth: mashed potatoes, stewed apples and black pudding), mustard soup and lamb stew with wild garlic are on the menu.

Pempelfort, *Nordstr. 53, Tel. (02 11) 4 98 13 61, daily 9am–12pm, cash only*

Jerónimos

Spanish or Portuguese; you don't have to decide; the cosy pub has both in wine and food. Inexpensive set-price lunches and daily specials make it difficult to choose.

Carlstadt, *Hohe Str. 23, Tel. (02 11) 6 00 32 86, Mon–Thu 10am–8pm, Fri 10am-10pm, Sat 11am–6pm*

Korea

Friendly restaurant with a whole range of Korean food: not only classics like marinated beef are prepared at the table but also beef tongue and spicy belly of pork. A must: Yuk-Que (raw minced beef Korean-style).

Stadtmitte, *Bismarckstr. 51, Tel. (02 11) 3 67 71 71, daily12pm–3pm and 5pm–11pm*

Kurhaus

In the Volksgarten park Manes Meckenstock (cabaret) has opened a charming pub with a small stage.

Bilk, *Auf'm Hennekamp 101, Tel. (02 11) 3 11 33 71, Wed-Sat 3pm–10pm, Sun 12am–9pm, cash only*

Nooij

The name sounds Asian, but Nooij, the chef has Dutch, Spanish and German forefathers. He serves an Asian-Mediterranean fusion. Breakfast, lunch and dinner: you sense the fantasy that inspires the chef.

Pegasos

Flingern, *Hoffeldstr. 37, Tel. (02 11) 6 98 66 89, daily 10am–1am (food till 11pm)*

Pegasos

Pegasos is a real Greek institution in Düsseldorf, decorated in turquoise and white. You can have assorted starters as a mixed dish; as main course have grilled fish, wonderful moussaka or tender meat.

Unterbilk, *Kirchfeldstr. 50, Tel. (02 11) 38 29 10, daily 12pm–12am*

Rote Laterne

The "laughing chef" dish makes you smile too because it is so tasty. The restaurant is different, there is no Chinese decoration and instead you have elegant design and authentic food. Its sister restaurant is "Rote Laterne".

Stadtmitte, *Kurfürstenstr. 29, Tel. (02 11) 8 30 22 83, daily 5.30pm–11.30pm, cash only*

Weinhaus Tanta Anna

Seoul

Hot and spicy soups. Koreans love it and so do the numerous Japanese guests who get there early in the evening. Traditional food, hot dishes and set-price menus with many small starters make it worthwhile.

- ***Unterbilk,*** *Kirchfeldstr. 59, Tel. (02 11) 3 19 06 48, Mon–Sat 12pm–2.30pm and 6pm–11pm, Sun 6pm–11pm*

Trattoria Emiliana

The chequered tablecloths and the uncomfortable benches simply belong to the place. But food is excellent, pizzas, lasagne and saltimbocca are nice and the daily menu in Italian is always worth studying.

- ***Pempelfort,*** *Adlerstr. 42, Tel. (02 11) 35 01 23, Mon–Fri 12pm–2.30pm and 6pm–11pm, Sat 6pm–11pm, cash only*

Weinhaus Tante Anna

Food and decoration are traditional. German food perpared and served in a modern way attracts locals and tourists.

- ***Altstadt,*** *Andreasstr. 2, Tel. (02 11) 13 11 63, Tue-Sat 6pm-1am*

MODERATE AND GOOD

Askitis

You can't tell from the outside that the Greek restaurant near the ice stadium has hidden treasures: the impressive wine cellar and the courtyard. Enjoy high-class Greek food in a stylish and absolutely authentic ambience.

- ***Düsseltal,*** *Herderstr. 73, Tel. (02 11) 6 02 07 13, Tue–Sat 6pm–12am, Sun 12pm–11pm (food 6pm–11pm)*

Baan Thai

It has been a classic among the Thai restaurants in the old part of the town for more than 30 years. Dining is excellent there. Specialities: crispy duck dishes. The starters served in small baskets are a must.

- ***Altstadt,*** *Berger Str. 28, Tel. (02 11) 32 63 63, daily 12pm–12am*

Baccala

Italian food at its best: four-course-menus, antipasti and of course dried cod in numerous varieties. Don't hesitate, special wishes are welcome. Tonino Iacovacci prepares best food.

- ***Mörsenbroich,*** *Heinrichstr. 83, Tel. (02 11) 6 18 26 42, Tue-Fri 12am-3pm and 6pm-11pm, Sat 6pm-11pm, Sun 12am-11pm*

Brasserie Stadthaus

French cuisine in a top-renovated historical building. Very attentive service. The coq au vin is just as good as the wines.

▮ *Altstadt, Mühlenstr. 31, Tel. (02 11) 16 09 28 15, Tue-Sat 12am-2.30pm, Mon-Sat 6pm-10.30pm*

Brand's Jupp

German new cuisine mixed with classics in a charming surrounding with paintings on the walls. In Stübchen (a small room) fresh fish is offered. Recommended: On Mondays try unexceptional varieties of Reibekuchen Rhineland-style (pancake made of grated potatoes).

▮ ***Wittlaer,*** *Kalkstr. 49, Tel. (02 11) 40 40 40, daily from 12pm)*

El Pescador

Name the fish and you (almost always) get it. And steaks, too. It's good, it's inexpensive and therefore always packed. It's not comfortable but the food is worth it.

▮ ***Flingern,*** *Grafenberger Allee 67, Tel. (02 11) 2 51 91 53, Tue–Sun 12pm–10pm*

Fischhaus

Mussels with dark bread (Rhineland-style), mussels with garlic Southern Europe-style: very delicious and a must during the months with an "r". You can even have them outside on the heated terrace. Fish dishes are freshly and tastily prepared and perfectly presented.

▮ ***Altstadt,*** *Berger Str. 3–7, Tel. (02 11) 8 54 98 64, daily 11.30am–12pm*

Kikaku

It's probably the best and the most typical Sushi restaurant in town with a wide choice of bite-size portions. Unusual to European taste are sea urchin and abalone - delicatessen in Japan.

▮ ***Stadtmitte,*** *Klosterstr. 38, Tel. (02 11) 35 78 53, Mo, Thu, Fri 12am-2pm, Mo-Fri/Sun 6pm-10pm Sun 6pm–10pm*

Kytaro

Spacious new makeover with excellent food: you don't find Gyros but refined Greek specialities at moderate prices. The waiters are well-dressed, competent and always charming.

▮ ***Flingern,*** *Grafenberger Allee 119, Tel. (02 11) 68 60 48, daily 11.30am–1am*

La Fenice

La Fenice not only has the name of the famous Venetian theatre, it is a theatre in itself with its masques, paintings and statues. Pasqualino Palmieris, once an Italian celebrity chef on the Kö, presents fabulous food theatre: excellent service and delicious desserts.

▮ ***Derendorf,*** *Ulmenstr. 122, Tel. (02 11) 32 94 11, Mon–Fri 12pm–2.30am and 6pm–11pm, Sat 5.30pm-11pm*

Las Palomas

If you want to try as many Spanish specialities as possible we recommend ordering a dish for two - which, by the way, is ample for three. Spanish guitar music, depending on the waiter's mood, is free.

Almost unheard of: you won't starve, even after midnight.

▪ ***Friedrichstadt,*** *Kirchfeldstr. 169, Tel. (02 11) 33 50 08, daily 6pm–3am*

Meuser

In the historical timbered house from 1641, Meuser follows the tradition in every respect. Not only the traditional Speckpfannkuchen (pancake with fried bacon), food on the menu is rich and very tasty.

▪ ***Niederkassel,*** *Alt-Niederkassel 75, Tel. (02 11) 55 12 72, daily 6pm–10pm*

Münstermanns Kontor

The name has been known to gourmets for generations: Münstermann sells delicatessen from all over the world. Typical European food which lets the ingredients do the work is served in the ambience of a French bistro.

▪ ***Carlstadt,*** *Hohe Str. 11, Tel. (02 11) 1 30 04 16, Tue–Fri 11am–10pm, Sat 11am–6pm*

Nakhon Thai

An unpretentious Thai restaurant; a wide range of food; little peppers symbolize how hot the food is. As starter try Nakhon Thai (bite-sizes like shrimps with rice noodles or little meat bags).

▪ ***Pempelfort,*** *Pempelforter Str. 45, Tel. (02 11) 3 61 38 70, daily 12pm–3pm and 6pm–12am*

Quintoo

Authentic Vietnamese cuisine in an unpretentious, but friendly-looking bistro. Offers a good variety of Mon-Kha-vi, which can be described as Vietnamese tapas. Traditional-style meals and street-food-snacks are available as well.

▪ ***Golzheim,*** *Kaiserswerther Str. 9, Tel. (02 11) 98 94 40 50*

Robert's Bistro

Years ago it was the only restaurant in the harbour. In those days people queued to get in and that hasn't changed. Robert's is in. Experts on French food enjoy fish soup, oysters or tongue of veal with foie gras.

- ***Unterbilk,*** *Wupperstr. 2, Tel. (02 11) 30 48 21, Tue–Fri 11.30am–11pm, Sat 10am–11pm, Bar Tue–Thu 5pm–1am, Fri/Sat 5pm–3am*

Sehrestaurant

In summer a day at Unterbacher See easily turns into a holiday. In the boathouse; a nice restaurant and a bar, home-made food. Recommended: brunch served at the sea bar on Sundays and public holidays.

- ***Unterbach,*** *Kleiner Torfbruch 31, Tel. (02 11) 20 13 91, daily from 10am, Sun/public holidays brunch from 10.30am*

Sichuan

Authentic Chinese food, a speciality is the Mongolian barbecue-buffet. The guests make their own choice of meat, fish and vegetables and the chef cooks them on a hot stone.

- ***Stadtmitte,*** *Am Wehrhahn 59, Tel. (02 11) 36 32 36, Mon–Fri 11.30am–3pm and 5.30pm–11pm Sat/Sun/public holidays 11.30am–11pm*

Tonhalle Kaiserwerth

This country-style restaurant offers a wide variety of traditional food with a modern touch. Meat clearly dominates the menu (try Mett, Flöns and Schweinshaxe), but vegetarians are not being neglected either (choice of pasta, salads or baked potatoes). The Altbier is freshly brewed in their subsidiary in Oberkassel.

- ***Kaiserswerth,*** *Clemensplatz 7, Tel. (02 11) 4 05 16 59, Mon-Sun 10 am - 1 am*

Tsun Gai

Dim Sum is Chinese and means delicious bite. In China you have them for breakfast or lunch. The Tsun Gai serves them in the evening as well, a good thing, too. They are delicious and rich.

- ***Stadtmitte,*** *Bahnstr. 72, Tel. (02 11) 35 42 91, Mon–Fri 11.30am–11pm, Sun 11.30am–11pm*

FOR GOURMETS

Fehrenbach

Elegant, minimalist, stylish and comfy: the restaurant of the Fehrenbach couple. The small but fine menu changes regularly. Try a set-price meal with German wine.

- ***Pempelfort,*** *Schwerinstr. 40, Tel. (02 11) 9 89 45 87, Tue–Sat from 6pm*

La Capannina

The classy Italian restaurant in a romantic courtyard is loved not only by the locals. Gourmets find what they are looking for, but at a price. A small but exquisite menu; speciality: rare fish.

- ***Oberkassel,*** *Hansaallee 30, Tel. (02 11) 55 26 72, Mon–Fri 12pm–2.30pm and 6pm–10.30pm, Sat 6pm–11pm, Sun 6pm–10.30pm*

La Terrazza

The name keeps its promise: high above Kö, the small but nice terrace belongs to one of the most beautiful in town with a fantastic view. Light Mediterranean food in a nice surrounding; expensive. If you are in for a treat, try it, you'll get what you are looking for.

- ***Stadtmitte,*** *Königsallee 30, Tel. (02 11) 32 75 40, Mon-Sat 11.30am-10pm, Sun 11.30am-2pm and 5.30pm-10pm*

Le Cheval Blanc

A gorgeous view of the gardens and stables from the restaurant; and astonishing and tasty food by Chef Michael Voll. Gourmets can trust him on a several-course-menu.

- ***Hubbelrath,*** *Mydlinghoven 4–10, Tel. (02 11) 40 13 00, Tue–Sun from 6pm*

Osteria Saitta

Italian high class food in a cosy little timber house: the brothers Saitta want to offer quality -not only with their fish dishes but as well with pasta and risotto. In the truffle season, pasta with Alba-truffle is an absolute must.

- ***Niederkassel,*** *Alt Niederkassel 32, Tel. (02 11) 57 49 34, Mon–Fri 12pm–3pm and 6pm–10.30pm, Sat 6pm–10.30pm*

Patrick's Seafood N°1

In the basement of this stylish designer house in the harbour Pino has created a somehow hidden paradise for friends of high-class Italian food. Italian hospitality and passionate chefs make you really feel at ease.

- ***Hafen,*** *Kaistr. 17, Tel. (02 11) 6 17 99 88, Mon-Sat 11.30-10pm, Sun 11.30am-10pm, Sun 11.30am-2pm and 5.30pm-10pm*

Piazza Saitta

Classy food: rare fish and seafood - lobster on wild garlic risotto, fried turbot with black truffle or a sweet and sour monkfish roast. Only the very best is served.

- ***Oberkassel,*** *Barbarossaplatz 3, Tel. (02 11) 1 71 51 91, Mon–Fri 12pm–3pm and 6pm–12am, Sat 12pm–12am*

Restaurant Schorn

Rhineland born Franz-Joseph Schorn is among the top-class chefs. The Düsseldorf Jong (boy from Düsseldorf) prepares Rhineland-style specialities on a top level. He is famous for his mustard roast: tradition on the one hand and French refinement on the other.

- ***Bilk,*** *Martinstr. 46a, Tel. (02 11) 3 98 19 72, Tue–Sat from 6pm*

Restaurant Schorn

Rosati/Rosati Due

For more than 30 years a classy Italian restaurant in a small street: Its starters from a cart were imitated by others. Specialities: fish and lamb fillet; a wide range of wine.

▮ ***Golzheim,*** *Felix-Klein-Str. 1, Tel. (02 11) 4 36 05 03, Sun–Fri 12am–11pm, Sat 5pm–11pm*

Rossini

A quick Italian meal – Rossini is the wrong address. Instead of pizza you get glazed wild duck and fillet of suckling-pig. Gourmets can have a perfect Italian night out.

▮ ***Pempelfort,*** *Kaiserstr. 5, Tel. (02 11) 49 49 94, daily 6pm–12pm*

Saltimbocca

This small but excellent restaurant is like a sitting-room. Asparagus or truffles or other rare foods are offered according to the season. But you shouldn't leave the restaurant without having tried the pasta.

▮ ***Gerresheim,*** *Kölner Tor 40, Tel. (02 11) 29 68 73, Tue–Sun 12am–2.30 pm and 6pm–12pm*

Sila Thai

This fine restaurant makes you pay dearly for the ambience and exclusivity; but you'll be rewarded: from hot to very hot curry; from tasty satays to crispy ducks – everything is recommendable even the papaya salad.

▮ ***Stadtmitte,*** *Bahnstr. 76, Tel. (02 11) 8 60 44 70, daily 12am–3pm and 6pm–1am*

PURE LUXURY

★ Berens am Kai

Holger Berens is a high-class chef. Hardly anyone is as imaginative and as outstanding as the native Westphalian. In his futuristic and stylish restaurant with view of the Rhine: you always bump into something spectacular.

▮ ***Hafen,*** *Kaistr. 16, Tel. (02 11) 3 00 67 50, Mon–Fri 12pm–2pm and 7pm–10pm , Sat 7pm–10pm*

Haus Stemberg

The family business combines rich, traditional and regional food with light modern varieties. Varieties of Matjes (young herring), piglet roast and sea bass on barley risotto are some of the numerous and excellent dishes.

▮ ***Velbert-Neviges,*** *Kuhlendahler Str. 295, Tel. (0 20 53) 56 49, Sat–Wed 12am–3pm and 6pm–11pm*

Herzog von Burgund

A stylish dinner in an intimate dark red ambience with candle light – sounds cosy. Austrian Erich Tiefenhaber specializes in modern and classic compositions. You feel the Viennese influence, not only eating Tafelspitz (cooked beef).

▮ ***Neuss,*** *Erftstr. 88, Tel. (0 21 31) 2 35 52, Tue–Fri 12am–2.30pm and 7pm–10pm, Sat 7pm–10pm*

Im Schiffchen

Jean-Claude Bougueil is king of the gourmet Mount Olympus. Behind the historical brick façade of the Schiffchen: culinary delights of

Im Schiffchen

French cuisine at their best. It has three stars. His lobster with camomile flowers has become a legend.

▌ ***Kaiserswerth,*** *Kaiserswerther Markt 9, Tel. (02 11) 40 10 50, Tue–Sat from 7pm*

Mönchenwerth

Imaginative food with an Asian touch: Guy de Vries and Christoph Schweinböck attract numerous gourmets with their fantastic creations; stylish surroundings for relaxation and in summer an idyllic beer garden.

▌ ***Meerbusch-Büderich,*** *Niederlöricker Str. 56, Tel. (0 21 32) 75 76 50, Tue–Sat 6pm–10pm, Sun 12pm–2.30pm and 6pm–10pm*

Nöthel's

Peter Noethel lost his two stars for re-opening his former "Hummerstübchen" under a new name, but the quality stayed the same. His lobster and seafood are exceptional and excellent; perfectly presented dishes, attentive service and elegant wines. Mind you, it's expensive.

▌ ***Lörick,*** *Bonifatiusstr. 35, Tel. (02 11) 59 44 02, Tue-Fri 12am-2pm and 6.30pm-10pm, Sat 6.30-10pm*

Tafelspitz 1876

Hanuta (a well-known German candy) made of foie gras or Hanuta as Baumkuchen (a cake of very thin layers) - these very imaginative dishes show 1star-chef Daniel Dal-Ben's creativity. His original compositions always bear a surprise: like Karree of Salzwiesenlamm (lamb fillet from lambs raised on salty meadows) or granulate of capers. It is expensive but you won't be disappointed.

▌ ***Düsseltal,*** *Grunerstr. 42a, Tel. (02 11) 1 71 73 61, Tue–Fri from 6.30pm*

Victorian

Round the corner from the Kö, the Victorian is the ideal place to make business while having an exceptional lunch. No need to worry: the unpretentious elegance of the fine menu won't change with the new 1star- owner. An attractive huge glass front.

▌ ***Stadtmitte,*** *Königstr. 3a, Tel. (02 11) 8 65 50 22, Bistro: Mon–Sun 11.30am-10.30pm, Restaurant: Tue-Sat 12am-2.30pm and 7pm-10.30pm*

VERY SWEET: CAFÉS

Bazzar

For coffee-addicts a must; in the shop expensive espresso-machines are sold and outside you enjoy your cappuccino. Tasty: freshly cut baguettes.

- ***Stadtmitte,*** *Heinrich-Heine-Allee 53, Tel. (02 11) 32 24 45, Mon–Sat 8am–11pm, So 10am–11pm*
- ***Flingern,*** *Schlüterstr. 3a, Tel. (02 11) 6 98 83 72, Mon–Fr 8am–8pm, Sat/So 10am–8pm*

Café Maushagen

Russian president Wladimir Putin was not the only one tempted by confectioner Georg Maushagen. His edible presents and the paradise birds made of sugar are known worldwide. Less prominent guests can enjoy his delicacies in the corner café.

- ***Pempelfort,*** *Jülicher Str. 9, Tel. (02 11) 46 47 48, Fri–Sun 10am–6pm, cash only*

Café Schuster

Ladies have their sherry at five o'clock, courting teenagers have a chocolate with frothed milk; the choice of cakes and biscuits is huge and for anyone not keen on sweets: quiches and Zwiebelkuchen (like a quiche with onions only) are freshly prepared.

- ***Kaiserswerth,*** *Klemensplatz 5, Tel. (02 11) 40 13 74, Mon–Fri 6.30am–7pm, Sat 6.30am–6pm, Sun 8am –7pm*

★ Heinemann

Heinemanns most famous fan is former Pope Benedikt, already when cardinal, he loved the cream cakes. No wonder - the recipes are family secrets. The founder of the café is said to be the creator of Herrentorte (cream cake in layers with brandy).

- ***Stadtmitte,*** *Martin-Luther-Platz 32, Tel. (02 11) 13 25 35, Mon–Fri 9am–7pm, Sat 9am–6.30pm, Sun 10am–6pm*
- ***Stadtmitte,*** *Bahnstr. 16, Tel. (02 11) 13 13 50, Mon–Fri 8.30am–6.30pm, Sat 8am–6pm, Sun 9.30am–6pm*

Heinemann

Kaffeepiraten

If you appreciate good coffee in different varieties together with lots of different items that belong to a good breakfast, take a break in this simply decorated, but welcoming café. Many guests enjoy a light meal or home-made cake while getting some work done.

▮ ***Bilk,*** *Neusser Str. 121, Mon-Fri 7am-7pm, Sat/Sun 10am-7pm*

Sugarbird Cupcakes

A true „girls' café" - the interior is all pink and white and the cupcakes almost too pretty to eat. Treat yourself with the lemon-, tiramisu- or Oreo-variety for example or enjoy a mint flavored latte. French style.

▮ ***Stadtmitte,*** *Heinrich-Heine-Allee 37, Tel. (0211) 56940733, Mon-Fri 10am-7pm, Sat 10am-8pm, Sun 10am-6pm*

BARS UND PUBS

Bar FiftyNine

This hotel bar is quite something. Mind you Robbie Williams flirted there in media-style. Even without celebrities, the bar of the first class hotel Interconti at Kö is busy. Düsseldorf trendies have their drinks there.

▮ ***Friedrichstadt,*** *Königsallee 59, Tel. (02 11) 82 85 12 10, Mon/Sun 12am-12pm, Tue-Thu 12am-1am, Fri/Sat from 12am*

Cubanitos

A typical cocktail bar: people regularly dance on the table in the late hours. It is because of the good ambience, swinging music and especially because of the drinks: The 120 mixed drinks are the best in town.

▮ ***Altstadt,*** *Kurze Str. 14, Tel. (02 11) 8 28 27 07, Mon–Thu/ Sun 6pm–1am, Fri/Sat 6pm–3am*

Ellingtons

Classical bar ambience of the forties: comfy leather armchairs, dimmed lights and dark walls. Background jazz music or live concerts.

▮ ***Friedrichstadt,*** *Scheurenstr. 5, Tel. (02 11) 3 11 39 00, Tue-Sun 8pm-3am, cash only*

Pardo Bar (in the K21 museum)

A bar for clubbers, trendies and art lovers: an in-meeting point. Museum café during the day, a nice restaurant with fusion food in the evening and a bar with 140 cocktails at weekends.

▮ ***Unterbilk,*** *Ständehausstr. 1 (K21), Tel. (02 11) 1 71 30 20, Tue–Thu 10am–7pm, Fri/Sat 10am–2am, So 10am–7pm*

Suco's do Brasil

A place for South America fans: samba music, South American waiters serve typical cocktails to their numerous compatriots in the courtyard of Wilhelm-Marx-Haus.

▮ ***Stadtmitte,*** *Kasernenstr. 6, Tel. (02 11) 13 26 50, Sun–Thu 10am–1am, Fri/Sat 10am–3am*

Tafelsilber

Restaurant, Cocktail Bar, and event location all in one huge room (and one smaller one) formerly known as Güterbahnhof Grafenberg, a train station for loading goods. Stylish interior and live music included. The food is a bit pricy, but delicious!

▮ ***Düsseltal,*** *Schlüterstr. 10, Tel. (02 11) 17 09 90 03*

Ufer 8

The concept: club with restaurant and terrace. Purist and minimalist interior; celebrities are said to dance there - some have already been seen; vocal house and disco-funk.

▮ ***Altstadt,*** *Rathausufer 8, Tel. (02 11) 2 00 56 76, Patio: Tue-Fri 4pm-12pm, Sat/Sun 12am-12pm*

CLUBS

Amber

Once the haunt of celebrities, the former Sam's had lost its glamour. Nevertheless, it is again becoming one of the places to go out to. Fine, but expensive.

▮ ***Stadtmitte,*** *Königsallee 27, Tel. (02 11) 32 81 71, Fri/Sat and before public holidays 11pm–open end www.amber-club.de*

Nachtresidenz

"Live the moment" is the official motto of the club. A big hall - the heart of the club - twelve metre-high-ceiling; beautiful people party there. The Kö is close, the outfits expensive; mainstream music.

▮ ***Stadtmitte,*** *Bahnstr. 13-15, Tel. (02 11) 1 36 57 55, Fri/Sat and before public holidays 10pm–5am*

Rudas Studios

Ideal for parties, events or live appearances: the fan community of this stylish club just keeps on growing.

▮ ***Hafen,*** *Kaistr. 7–9, Tel. (02 11) 69 55 69 90, for opening hours check www.rudasstudios.com*

Stahlwerk

Concert hall and comedy stage during the week, and place for parties at the weekend. On Fridays and Saturdays, there are dance parties in the former steelworks. Parties of the 80s or 90s have become legendary; alternative music at "Dungeon Day".

▮ ***Flingern,*** *Ronsdorfer Str. 134, Tel. (02 11) 73 03 50, Fri/Sat and before holidays from 10pm, for further opening hours check www.stahlwerk.de, cash only*

Port Seven

Event- and party-location in one of Düsseldorf's most fancy area - the media harbour. Professional hosting of concerts and club events for young people.

▮ ***Hafen,*** *Franziusstr. 7, Tel. (02 11) 30 33 09 99, check www.port-seven.de for events*

Königsallee – the famous shopping mile

SHOPPING IN DÜSSELDORF

Forget the clichés about "Shopping in Düsseldorf". The **Königsallee (Kö)** definitely is a most trendy shopping mile for the rich and the beautiful, for stars and starlets: an all-year-open catwalk event with choice designer shops. It is a consumerist delight to watch the glamour and showing-off. Fortunately, young and creative designers have set up shop in the neighbourhood.

The **Kö,** the nearby **Schadowstraße** and, of course, the **Altstadt** and **Carlstadt** have a lot to offer and make your heart beat faster. Especially Carlstadt with its exceptional architectural flair is a real treasurey trove of small and extravagant shops with a very special flair. To go on a spending spree around here you need serious money to pay the horrendous prices, but then you don't shop here because you need something. Follow Coco Chanel's maxim: spend your money well, don't buy many things, just an extravagant little something; if not for every day then for a special occasion.

In less known shopping streets you'll find exceptional clothes moderately priced; for example **Ackerstraße** in Flingern; it goes on for ever and in its beginnings near the main station, shops are rather plain but with increasing house numbers they become more attractive. Quite a few small, remarkable and individual shops; their designers don't follow the fashion mainstream and cosumers can watch them work. Round the corner **Ackerstraße/Hermannstraße** you'll find the cosy little bistros and cafés you look for in vain in the city centre where bistros and cafés often belong to chains.

Like Ackerstraße **Collenbachstraße** in Pempelfort has become an attractive street in recent years when hunting for exceptional and budget-priced fashions. A stone's throw away is frantic **Nordstraße** with oddball shops for everyday shopping and many appealing boutiques. Equally busy and worth a visit are **Rethelstraße** in Düsseltal, **Benderstraße** in Gerresheim, **Hauptstraße** in Ben-

TIPS

Beyermann Goldschmiede
An oasis for fans of fine stationery and jewellery in a studio run by several artists.
➲page 78

Börgermann
Impressive choice of well-shaped kitchen, pocket and hunters' knives. ➲page 78

Franzen
The big names for china, glass and silverware are represented there. ➲page 79

Düsseldorfer Senfladen
Museum and shop: a real paradise for those who love the traditional local mustard.
➲page 93

At the Corneliusplatz

rath, **Kaiserswerther Markt, Klemensplatz** in quiet Kaiserswerth, **Lorettostraße** in Bilk and **Luegallee** in Oberkassel. Long-established and new shops in those busy and charming streets tend to be real treasure troves for shopping.

So, forget the cliché about "Shopping in Düsseldorf". Not only the city centre but as well the districts are good for shopping.

ART OF LIVING

Art Maroc

Browsing there is like being in another world: The world of fabulous antique Kelims, artfully decorated furniture and colourful ceramics. The shop is so big and the assortment so huge you won't leave the shop without having bought a Moroccan craft object.

- ***Flingern,*** *Ackerstr. 19, Tel. (02 11) 1 64 04 80*

★ Beyermann Goldschmiede

A haven for fans of fine stationery and jewellery in a studio run by several artists: Goldsmith Isabel Beyermann designs fine jewellery and bookbinder Jan Adolphs individual book covers, beautiful calligraphy articles are featured.

- ***Flingern,*** *Hermannstr. 28, Tel. (02 11) 67 15 31, www.blattgold-duesseldorf.de*

★ Börgermann

The choice of well-shaped kitchen, pocket and hunters' knives is impressive. Scissors and kitchen utensils are featured. Hunters and collectors will find precious handmade pieces and a wide range of Swiss army knives. Börgermann is indeed a specialist in cutting utensils.

- ***Altstadt,*** *Berger Str. 15, Tel. (02 11) 13 12 55, www.boergermann.de*

Cucinaria

High-quality gadgets for cooking, eating and drinking are big sellers. Proforma has the furniture and Cucinaria the gadgets made of high-grade steel, ceramics and china.

- ***Carlstadt,*** *Carlsplatz 14–15, Tel. (02 11) 88 28 72 10, www.cucinaria-duesseldorf.de*

Fausel, Biskamp

In former times it was a plain wallpaper shop. If you need a new interior decor concept, go there. You'll get good advice and professional help. Classic or modern, top-quality is guaranteed.

- ***Stadtmitte,*** *Kasernenstr. 6, Tel. (02 11) 97 76 30, www.fauselbiskamp.de*

Fleamarkets

- ***Bilk,*** *Aachener Straße, every Saturday from 8am, Live Music in Café Sperrmüll, www.troedelmarkt-aachenerplatz.de*
- ***Derendorf,*** *Großmarkt-Gelände, Ulmenstr. 275, every second Saturday in the month*

☆ Franzen

All the nice things of this world under one roof: A paradise for traditionalists and modern design fans; the big names for china, glass and silverware and the leading accessories and interior décor collections are represented.

- ***Stadtmitte,*** *Königsallee 42, Tel. (02 11) 13 07 80, www.franzen.de*

Gute N8!

"Good night" is a suitable name for this beautifully decorated shop. It is anything but a plain shop where you can buy mattresses; only luxurious bits and pieces for your bedroom are on sale. You get very friendly and competent help.

- ***Carlstadt,*** *Hohe Str. 46, Tel. (02 11) 32 33 01, www.guten8.com*

Kyoto

Japanese culture is thought to be minimalist, but there are quite exceptional accessories. In this specialised shop on Japanese interior décor the consumer will have problems to choose: fans, lacquered items, ceramics, house wear and wooden shoes.

- ***Stadtmitte,*** *Immermannstr. 26, Tel. (02 11) 35 27 36*

Lambert

This fine furniture and accessories shop is always worth a visit. You can have coffee in the foyer, of course from cups you can buy. The cosy atmosphere is inviting for a leisurely study of the tasteful assortment.

- ***Stadtmitte,*** *Stilwerk, Grünstr. 15, Tel. (02 11) 86 20 42 29, www.lambert-home.de*

Licht im Raum

If you are at your wits' end as to what to do with your lighting, this is the place to go to. Experts there first think in qualities of lighting and then in nice designs. The assortment includes the well known modern brands of lamps.

- ***Friedrichstadt,*** *Graf-Adolf-Str. 49, Tel. (02 11) 99 40 00, www.licht-im-raum.de*

Manufactum Store

Manufactum sells useful gadgets and décor made of classic material. Furniture, toys or dishes are made of environmentaly safe material; they last long and are easy to repair. Next door is brot&butter (bread and butter); these are good-quality agricultural produce.

- ***Stadtmitte,*** *Steinstr. 4, Tel. (02 11) 6 02 08 88, www.manufactum.de*

Marx Antik
Antiques, rarities and odd things on 300 square metres: owner Klaus-Günther Marx has specialized in antique shop fittings; he also sells individual items to private persons. You can lease his legendary deco props.

- ***Stadtmitte,*** *Worringer Str. 70, Tel. (02 11) 9 35 78 42*
- ***Wersten,*** *Kölner Landstr. 375, Tel. (02 11) 75 82 82, www.naund-marxmoebel-duesseldorf.de*

Muji-Store
This modest low-price Japanese-style shop got an award from the German association of retail shops: best shop for Lifestyle and Living. Not surprising: interior décor and clothes are of appealing design and moderately-priced.

- ***Stadtmitte,*** *Kö-Galerie, Königsallee 60–62, Tel. (02 11) 8 60 66 61, www.muji.eu*

Roche-Bobois
This extravagant French furniture store satisfies any given taste on two floors: Provonçal country-house style, funky modern or Asian minimalist: everything is tasteful and of high quality.

- ***Stadtmitte,*** *Stilwerk, Grünstr. 15, Tel. (02 11) 8 63 26 40, www.roche-bobois.com*

Wandel
Armchairs, writing-desks or a complete coffee-house style interior; Markus Wildhagen collects exceptional interior objects. Furniture of the last 100 years, of the 50s and 70s, and especially art deco and art nouveau are sold on 900 square metres.

- ***Stadtmitte,*** *Worringer Str. 57, Tel. (02 11) 90 15 87-12, www.wandel-einrichtungsobjekte.de*

Who's perfect?
Design-fans can choose among 2,000 design giveaways of big brands like Arketipo, Bonaldo, Cattelan or ICF. Exhibits and high-fashion facsimiles of famous designers are moderately-priced.

- ***Stadtmitte,*** *Immermannstr. 12, Tel. (02 11) 16 88 87 40, www.whos-perfect.de*

BEAUTY

Calendula
A specialist shop with an excellent selection of natural cosmetics stocks the leading brands: Weleda, Dr. Hauschka and Sante. It features creams, shampoos, oils as well as fancy cosmetics, hair dyes, spices, teas and accessories for body care.

- ***Pempelfort,*** *Nordstr. 2b, Tel. (02 11) 37 86 55, www.calendula-naturkosmetik.de*

Haartiste
Clients love the stylish atmosphere and the perfect hair cuts. Owner Solange Caillau gets her ideas from the nearby academy of arts and produces real works of art. Haartiste is not a snobbish hairdresser's but a friendly and modern place for women and men.

- ***Altstadt,*** *Mühlengasse 6, Tel. (02 11) 8 62 95 80, www.haartiste.de*

Marlies Möller
A perfectly styled salon in the elegant Sevens Gallery: Top stylist Marlies Möller is trend setter with her typical dry cut technique.
- ***Stadtmitte,*** *Sevens, Königsallee 56, Tel. (02 11) 5 22 87 40, www.marliesmoeller.de*

Schminklädchen
Top address for event-make-up, effect-make-up and camouflage: owner Marianne Windisch offers whatever you need in make-up or accessories for a glamorous appearance. In workshops you can learn how to create your own make-up.
- ***Unterbilk,*** *Bilker Allee 46, Tel. (02 11) 39 18 50*

Schnitzler
Schnitzler is most famous among the rich and the beautiful, even Isabella Rosselini was there. Brands and service are just top. In the Shiseido Beauty Lounge you can have a treatment and make-up for free.
- ***Stadtmitte,*** *Schadow Arkaden, Schadowstr. 11, Tel. (02 11) 3 23 08 01; Shiseido Beauty Lounge, Tel. (02 11) 3 23 08 02*
- ***Stadtmitte,*** *Sevens, Königsallee 56, Tel. (02 11) 37 04 0*
- ***Stadtmitte,*** *Breidenbacher Hof, Königsallee 11, Tel. (02 11) 68 78 74 14, www.parfuemerie-schnitzler.de*

ENTERTAINMENT

A & O Medien Store
A good address: a wide assortment and imaginative displays: no searching around: CDs, records, music books and magazines, DVDs of old and new films.
- ***Stadtmitte,*** *Schadow Arkaden, Schadowstr. 11, Tel. (02 11) 8 60 60 49, www.aundo-medien.de*

Apple Store
Open-plan Showroom with the latest apple products to test. Skilled and friendly service.
- ***Stadtmitte,*** *Kö-Bogen, Königsallee 2, Tel. (02 11) 42 47 06 00 www.apple.com*

Hifi-Referenz
A top-class high-fidelity shop with excellent service and products. It features a wide choice of top-quality hi-fi and high-end-products. You can test your favourite stereo equipment or parts of it in a studio.
- ***Stadtmitte,*** *Steinstr. 31, Tel. (02 11) 32 51 52, www.hifi-referenz.de*

Leistenschneider
This specialized photo shop has a long tradition in the heart of Düsseldorf; it was founded more than a hundred years ago. Being the leading shop it has a wide assortment of photo and video equipment. This is the place if you are looking for a digital camera. There are also second-hand offers.
- ***Stadtmitte,*** *Schadow Arkaden, Schadowstr. 11, Tel. (02 11) 13 00 50*

DEPARTMENT STORES

Breuninger

- **Stadtmitte,** *Königsallee 2, Tel. (02 11) 56 64 10*

C & A

- **Bilk,** *Düsseldorf Arcaden, Friedrichstr. 133, Tel. (02 11) 99 45 94 27*
- **Stadtmitte,** *Schadowstr. 77–79, Tel. (02 11) 1 60 80, www.cunda.de*

Carsch-Haus

- **Stadtmitte,** *Heinrich-Heine-Platz 1, Tel. (02 11) 8 39 70, www.galeria-kaufhof.de*

Galeria Kaufhof

- **Stadtmitte,** *Am Wehrhahn 1, Tel. (02 11) 1 60 30, www.galeria-kaufhof.de*
- **Stadtmitte,** *Königsallee 1–9, Tel. (02 11) 1 39 10*

Karstadt

- **Stadtmitte,** *Schadowstr. 93, Tel. (02 11) 3 68 60, www.karstadt.de*

Peek & Cloppenburg

- **Stadtmitte,** *Berliner Allee 1, Tel. (02 11) 86 70 60, www.peekundcloppenburg.de*

FASHION

American Apparel

The colourful products of the biggest American producer of T-shirts are the incarnation of cool understatements. According to the producer all shirts are produced in high-wage California. He doesn't use any logos or propaganda.

- ***Stadtmitte,*** *Königsallee 90, Tel. (02 11) 3 01 43 78, www.americanapparel.net*

Anziehung

Sabine Hennig sells casual fashion for every day from Turnover, Expresso, Mania and many more. Friendly service and moderate prices; a shop to browse in, furniture of teakwood and interior accessories are as well on sale.

- ***Pempelfort,*** *Schwerinstr. 5, Tel. (02 11) 1 59 45 88, www.anziehung-lifestyle.de*

Atelier Headwig

The eternal hunt for a perfect handbag: at Christin Dahlmann's you should find what you're after. In her courtyard studio she creates unique items to order in every design and colour. She prefers fabrics like felt, lamb's nappa, goatskin leather, cow's nappa or wild-animal pelts.

- ***Pempelfort,*** *Tußmannstr. 70, Tel. (02 11) 5 14 24 03, www.headwig.de*

Atelier Ursbob

The number of the building is important here, as Ulla Meiners has refrained from using any lettering. She creates fashion for women who want original clothes. Fresh colours, slim outline, precise cuts, fine cloth and flashy details characterize her models.

- ***Flingern,*** *Hermannstr. 33, Tel. (02 11) 6 99 96 96, www.ursbob.de*

BeckerHarbort Collections

The small shop is readily underestimated but most people know about the high-quality clothes for everyday wear: Friendly atmosphere, fashion from Backstage, Turnover or Personal Affairs, elegant and not overdone too stylish.

- ***Oberkassel,*** *Luegallee 126, Tel. (02 11) 5 56 02 67*

Anke Rettich

Düsseldorf has got a race track, so attractive hats are a must. Whether you bet on horses or not, hat designer Anke Rettich offers extravagant hats for every occasion. She helps you to design your individual hat in her shoroom.

- ***Bilk,*** *Suitbertusstr. 26, , Tel. (0 15 73) 6 20 94 16, www.anke-rettich.de*

Filz

Barbara Kessler has got caps, hats, egg warmer, bags with handles, or baby shoes – useful and nice things made of felt. Choose among a wide assortment or place an order. During opening hours the designer willingly shows you how felt is made and what you can do with it.

DESIGNERS' LABELS

AIGNER
▮ **Stadtmitte,** *Königsallee 60, Tel. (02 11) 3 23 09 55, www.aignermunich.com*

Armani
▮ **Stadtmitte,** *Königsallee 72, Tel. (02 11) 86 63 00, www.giorgioarmani.com*

Bogner
▮ **Stadtmitte,** *Königsallee 6–8, Tel. (02 11) 13 42 22, www.bogner.de*

Bree
▮ **Stadtmitte,** *Schadowstr. 11, Tel. (02 11) 1 37 30 60, www.bree.de*

Burberry
▮ **Stadtmitte,** *Königsallee 50, Tel. (02 11) 32 09 26, www.burberry.com*

Chanel
▮ **Stadtmitte,** *Königsallee 30, Tel. (02 11) 32 59 92, www.chanel.com*

Gucci
▮ **Stadtmitte,** *Königsallee 40, Tel. (02 11) 8 63 28 10, www.gucci.com*

Hermès
▮ **Stadtmitte,** *Königsallee 27, Tel. (02 11) 86 43 80, www.hermes.com*

Hugo Boss
▮ **Stadtmitte,** *Königsallee 13, Tel. (02 11) 21 07 51 70, www.hugoboss.com*

Jil Sander
▮ **Stadtmitte,** *Königsallee 62, Tel. (02 11) 32 84 44, www.jilsander.com*

Joop
▮ **Stadtmitte,** *Königsallee 56, Tel. (02 11) 8 68 14 41, www.joop.com*

Lacoste
▮ **Stadtmitte,** *Königsallee 60, Tel. (02 11) 8 36 84 43, www.lacoste.de*

Louis Vuitton
▮ **Stadtmitte,** *Königsallee 20, Tel. (02 11) 32 32 300, www.louisvuitton.com*

Mandarina Duck
▮ **Stadtmitte,** *Königsallee 56, Tel. (02 11) 32 40 80, www.mandarinaduck.com*

Marc Cain
▮ **Stadtmitte,** *Königsallee 21–23, Tel. (02 11) 1 35 35 40, www.marc-cain.com*

Max Mara
▮ **Stadtmitte,** *Königsallee 4, Tel. (02 11) 8 60 69 80, www.maxmara.com*

Prada
▮ **Stadtmitte,** *Königsallee 34a, Tel. (02 11) 86 57 80, www.prada.com*

René Lezard
▮ **Stadtmitte,** *Schadowstr. 11, Tel. (02 11) 3 23 72 10, www.rene-lezard.com*

Strenesse
▮ **Stadtmitte,** *Königsallee 56, Tel. (02 11) 86 32 23 70, www.strenesse.com*

Tod's
▮ **Stadtmitte,** *Königsallee 12, Tel. (02 11) 8 54 97 44, www.todsgroup.com*

Tommy Hilfiger
▮ **Stadtmitte,** *Schadowstr. 14, Tel. (02 11) 8 28 59 85, www.tommyhilfiger.de*

Versace
▮ **Stadtmitte,** *Königsallee 21-23, Tel. (02 11) 8 62 93 50, www.versace.com*

Windsor
▮ **Stadtmitte,** *Königsallee 2, Tel. (02 11) 8 36 87 07, www.windsor.ch*

■ ***Derendorf,*** *Collenbachstr. 31, Tel. (02 11) 5 14 46 01, www.perlfisch.de*

Identità Italiana

A cool shop without frills and pomp; young Italian fashion from Patrizia Pepe, Daniele Lessandri and co. You won't find many every day clothes, but loads of extravagancies for exclusive events. Highly-priced.

■ ***Altstadt,*** *Carlsplatz 22, Tel. (02 11) 8 69 30 88 www.identita-italiana.de*

Ingrid Homberg

Women who prefer classic clothes have to go to Ingrid Homberg. A well chosen assortment of expensive fashion made of fine cloth and of elegant and timeless style. A highlight are the temptingly beautiful leather coats and lambskin jackets.

■ ***Düsseltal,*** *Rethelstr. 172, Tel. (02 11) 62 62 88,*

Kleidsam

Nice atmosphere, moderately priced, funny accessories - this small shop opposite Bilker church is a paradise for individualists. Sandra Dhingra carefully selects different trendy labels: Noa Noa, Hooch, Roxy and Spoon.

■ ***Unterbilk,*** *Neusser Str. 123, Tel. (02 11) 3 03 38 60, www.kleidsam.eu*

Mandalay

Stylist Nathalie Flörke emphazises good advice. She specializes in wearable but original fashion and chooses from collections of Noa Noa, Stills, drykorn and aem-key; Schiesser revival lingerie is a perfect dream to go with the clothes.

■ ***Derendorf,*** *Collenbachstr. 41, Tel. (02 11) 9 53 58 75, www.mandalay-shop.com*

Norman Icking

For decades the native Westphalian, Norman Icking, has been part of the fashion scene in Düsseldorf. His partner, Ruth Heinen, designs matter-of-fact fashion to wear at work, beautiful party dresses with sex-appeal and breath-taking evening dresses of velvet and silk.

■ ***Stadtmitte,*** *Kasernenstr. 6, Tel. (02 11) 13 13 17, www.norman-icking.de*

Peter O. Mahler

Fashion is all black to him, total purism devoid of all colour. That's what's made him famous in Düsseldorf and beyond.

■ ***Carlstadt,*** *Bastionstr. 33, Tel. (02 11) 86 72 20, www.peter-o-mahler.de*

Petra Glatz

Petra Glatz has stuck to her philosophy for years: no frills and slim lines characterize her models. Friends of reduced linen clothes and nice fabrics should go there in summer. You'll find homely interior accessories as well.

■ ***Carlstadt,*** *Hohe Str. 17 Tel. (02 11) 21 07 37 02*

Shanghai Chinese Lifestyle

Fashion city Düsseldorf goes Asian: classic, slim, figure-accentuated dresses with slits on both sides and small stand-up collars are sold from 120 euro. Owner Xiaoming Thiess-Wang wants to introduce kimonos and house wear as well.

- ***Stadtmitte,*** *Immermannstr. 27, Tel. (02 11) 35 74 06*

Uli Knecht

Fashion labels like Sabine Schumacher for women are found on the first floor and more than just the basics for men on the ground floor. The former classic range has given way to greater elegance and spirit.

- ***Stadtmitte,*** *Königstr. 3, Tel. (02 11) 32 46 52, www.uliknecht.de*

Wolf Sieger

You'll find speciality goods not only in the city of Düsseldorf. Away from the big shopping streets Wolf Sieger stands his ground with top-class design of Versace and Dolce & Gabbana: the place to go to for fashion-conscious women and men.

- ***Pempelfort,*** *Venloer Str. 2/corner Nordstr., Tel. (02 11) 49 49 14*

Zarah Barnabas

It is a very fine address for fans of fashion avant-garde style as created by Vivienne Westwood, Helmut Lang and Alexander McQueen. Owner and designer Britta Schoeler designs highly feminine dresses and stylish tops under the label of Afterschock.

- ***Altstadt,*** *Carlsplatz 4, Tel. (02 11) 32 48 78*

LINGERIE

Bornemeyer

Local top address for tights and lingerie. The assortment is up-to-date and expertise assistants only sell what really fits.

- ***Stadtmitte,*** *Schadowstr. 73, Tel. (02 11) 35 35 81, www.bornemeyer.de*

Calida Store

Fine quality lingerie for men, women and kids. Comfortable and trendy collections including beachwear and loungewear.

- ***Stadtmitte,*** *Blumenstar. 7, Tel. (02 11) 2 00 59 41, www.calida-shop.de*

Claudia Rüdinger

Not every day underwear, high-quality lingerie from leading brands like La Perla, Malizia or Donna Karan: Düsseldorf's women shop at Claudia Krüger's. The shop was founded 25 years ago and during summer the latest swim wear is on sale.

- ***Stadtmitte,*** *Immermannstr. 22, Tel. (02 11) 35 31 21*
- ***Stadtmitte,*** *Steinstr. 20, Tel. (02 11) 8 63 24 88*
- ***Stadtmitte,*** *Kö-Galerie, Königsallee 60, Tel. (02 11) 16 25 45*

Heike Siemes

If you are not that keen on luxurious lace keep this address in mind: high quality and simply cut lingerie from Malizia, Mary Jo, Joop and Toni Gard.

▪ ***Flingern,*** *Ackerstr. 203,*
Tel. (02 11) 67 16 45
www.siemes-dessous.de

Mohnfeld-Moden

Don't be irritated by the old-fashioned writing on the façade, Mohnfeld is one of the best assorted lingerie shops in town. Night wear for women and men, tights and socks and stylish underwear, you name it and you'll find it.

▪ ***Carlstadt,*** *Hohe Str. 21,*
Tel. (02 11) 32 87 31,
www.mohnfeld-moden.de

SECOND HAND

Check out

A treasure trove of exclusive designer fashion and accessories for women. All the important labels like Chanel, Hermes, Gucci and Prada are there. And assistants are friendly even if you don't look a seriously rich fashion victim.

▪ ***Pempelfort,*** *Blücherstr. 24,*
Tel. (02 11) 44 55 44
www.checkout-duesseldorf.de

Couture 2nd

This exquisite shop pays homage to Coco Chanel who once said: "A well-cut dress suits every woman". Suits, dresses, jewellery and shoes in typical black and white design recall Chanel history. Find other classy brands as well.

▪ ***Carlstadt,*** *Hohe Str. 20,*
Tel. (02 11) 5 69 42 61,
www.couture2nd.de

Mae's second hand deluxe

Mae Würth only sells pieces that have been worn once or twice. Label-conscious customers shop there for business-outfits and evening dresses and pay much less than the original price: Armani, Chanel, Yves Laurent and many more.

▪ ***Oberkassel,*** *Cheruskerstr. 56,*
Tel. (02 11) 58 83 49,

SHOES

Brooker

The right place for perfect shoes: Brooker has the newest models from leading brands like Prada, Miu Miu, Jil Sander and Puma. All you need is enough money.

▪ ***Stadtmitte,*** *Bahnstr. 16,*
Tel. (02 11) 13 34 04

Edward's

You know a gentleman by his shoes: hand-sewn and of classic style. You'll need 300 euro to spare, but it's an investment that can last forever. A wide choice of fine leather ware is also on sale.

▪ ***Stadtmitte,*** *Kö-Galerie, Königsallee 60, Tel. (02 11) 32 06 34,*
www.edwards-herrenschuhe.de

Görtz

Women and men find top-fashionable shoes and boots moderately priced in the different branches. Their own label Görtz 17 is featured as well as Boss, Lloyd; sneakers from Nike, Hilfiger, Lacoste and Puma.

DESIGNER OUTLET

Lieblingsstücke

The name of Susann Weipert's attractive shop translates as "favourite pieces" and offers a good selection in a now trendy part of the Flingern district. A beautifully decorated boutique and a must for women seeking original and interesting second-hand garments.

- ***Flingern,*** *Bruchstr. 1/corner Lindenstr., Tel. (02 11) 6 99 93 67, www.lieblings-stuecke.de*

YOUNG FASHION

Benetton

- ***Stadtmitte,*** *Königsallee 66, Tel. (02 11) 8 63 24 20, www.benetton.com*

Cinque

- ***Carlstadt,*** *Benrather Str. 12, Tel. (02 11) 13 06 59 70, www.cinque.de*

Diesel

- ***Carlstadt,*** *Kasernenstr. 1, Tel. (02 11) 8 62 29 66, www.diesel.com*

Esprit

- ***Bilk,*** *Friedrichstr. 133, Tel. (02 11) 73 27 62 80*
- ***Stadtmitte,*** *Schadowstr. 17–21, Tel. (02 11) 1 59 79 70, www.esprit.de*

Hallhuber

- ***Stadtmitte,*** *Königsallee 22, Tel. (02 11) 2 10 79 57, www.hallhuber.de*
- ***Altstadt,*** *Flinger Str. 27, Tel. (02 11) 3 23 88 20, www.mango.com*

- ***Stadtmitte,*** *Kö-Galerie, Königsallee 60, Tel. (02 11) 32 71 92*
- ***Stadtmitte,*** *Heinrich-Heine-Platz 1, Tel. (02 11) 32 87 00*
- ***Stadtmitte,*** *Konrad-Adenauer-Platz 14 (main station), Tel. (02 11) 8 30 23 20, www.goertz-shop.de*

Prange

There are two branches of this family-owned shop on the Königsallee, number 28 offers elegant and classic shoes, number 48 stands for top-modern and exclusive shoes made for luxury women. On the first floor men and children are looked after.

- ***Stadtmitte,*** *Königsallee 28, Tel. (02 11) 3 61 52 52*
- ***Stadtmitte,*** *Königsallee 48, Tel. (02 11) 3 61 51 43*

Schuhmacherei Pans

Silvia and Dirk Pans do more than just repair shoes - new soles, new heels. You can have your shoes made to measure and you can even have your leather handbag made.

- ***Benrath,*** *Börchemstr. 36, Tel. (02 11) 7 10 38 40, www.schuhmacherei-pans.de*

Schuhwiese

Good selection of "natural" shoes: good to look at and comfortable to wear – a very rare combination when it comes to shoes.

- ***Altstadt,*** *Kapuzinergasse 3–5, Tel. (02 11) 8 54 90 34, www.schuhwiese.de*

HOBBY

Bunert

In for running? Professional, amateur, long-distance runner, jogger, and sprinter or cross-country runner: you should find what you're after. The assistants themselves are runners and provide you with loads of good tips from experience.

▮ ***Derendorf,*** *Roßstr. 69,*
Tel. (02 11) 61 48 60,
www.bunert.de

Golf House

Germany's largest golf equipment dealer offering clubs and trolleys as well as golf fashion.

▮ ***Stadtmitte,*** *Bahnstr. 3,*
Tel. (0211) 323601
www.golfhouse.de

K + M, Kunst und Material

A nice little shop; artists should find what they are after: brushes, handmade paper, easels and passe-partout cutters. Not only art students, hobby painters and friends of fine paper browse there.

▮ ***Altstadt,*** *Altestadt 13,*
Tel. (02 11) 32 88 77

Menzels Lokschuppen

Meeting point for electric train fans: Limited special models, carefully made model houses and detailed landscapes and of course specialist's literature for browsing and study.

▮ ***Friedrichstadt,*** *Friedrichstr. 6,*
Tel. (02 11) 37 33 28,
www.menzels-lokschuppen.de

Marc O'Polo

▮ ***Stadtmitte,*** *Königsallee 13,*
Tel. (02 11) 21 07 26 78
▮ ***Stadtmitte,*** *Königsallee 52,*
Tel. (02 11) 13 41 18,
www.marc-o-polo.com

Replay

▮ ***Stadtmitte,*** *Heinrich-Heine-Allee 53, Tel. (02 11) 1 37 32 88,*
www.replay.de

Stefanel

▮ ***Stadtmitte,*** *Königsallee 40,*
Tel. (02 11) 2 10 70 36,
www.stefanel.ro

S.Oliver

▮ ***Altstadt,*** *Flinger Str. 50,*
Tel. (02 11) 83 68 05 10
▮ ***Bilk,*** *Friedrichstr. 133,*
Tel. (02 11) 30 12 17 93,
www.soliver.com

Tom Tailor

▮ ***Stadtmitte,*** *Königsallee 14,*
Tel. (02 11) 8 63 25 60,
www.tom-tailor.com

Zara

▮ ***Altstadt,*** *Flinger Str. 28,*
Tel. (02 11) 86 32 44 40
▮ ***Stadtmitte,*** *Schadowstr. 15,*
Tel. (02 11) 8 36 82 26
▮ ***Stadtmitte,*** *Königsallee 64,*
Tel. (02 11) 8 28 29 29,
www.zara.com

Purzel-Baum

Specialist for natural and clever toys. The assortment is chosen strictly by social and ecological standards. Sounds strict, don't be afraid of playing, fun and joy of life are an important part of the programme.

- ***Flingern,*** *Birkenstr. 86, Tel. (02 11) 1 64 06 03, www.purzel-baum.com*

Spielschiff

A nice little shop and a carefully chosen assortment of toys made from natural materials. You won't find ball games and hardly any plastic. Gift wrappings are a dream. The assistants are experts and take their time.

- ***Pempelfort,*** *Kaiserswerther Str. 6, Tel. (02 11) 4 98 36 01, www.spielschiff.de*

Tennis & Ski

Rainer Adams was the first tennis trainer to get the A-licence of the German tennis association in Düsseldorf. He has owned his specialized shop for more than 20 years. Professional know-how is guaranteed. A wide range of rackets, skis and a ski repair service are featured.

- ***Oberkassel,*** *Luegallee 136, Tel. (02 11) 58 81 82, www.tennis-und-ski.de*

INDULGENCE

Bakery my heart

The Japanese quarter round the Immermannstraße offers a lot food wise. In a neat corner shop with a not very Japanese name: "Bakery my heart" you'll find tempting Japanese bakery products. But you'll also get simple banana cake and savoury rolls, filled with scrambled eggs or potato salad.

- ***Stadtmitte,*** *Marienstr. 26, Tel. (02 11) 5 50 47 60*

Basic Bio-Supermarkt

This supermarket is a good example: organic food is fashionable. You get all you need for your daily needs and can choose from a high variety. The whole grain bakery offers cakes and savoury snacks.

- ***Unterbilk,*** *Friedrichstr. 73, Tel. (02 11) 88 29 30 00, www.basicbio-genuss-fuer-alle.de*

Der Spirituosenladen

An old and well-established speciality shop for alcohol in a lane in the old city: the range, including rarities is phenomenal: cognac, champagne, whisky (about 450 brands) liquors, schnapps and several brands of rum. If you need something they haven't got, no problem, they'll find it for you.

- ***Altstadt,*** *Kapuzinergasse 8, Tel. (02 11) 1 37 30 89, www.spirituosen-vonhalasz.de*

El Martin

You needn't have a bad conscience buying there. All products offered are fair trade. The wafer-thin biological plain chocolates are delicious. Tea, coffee and decorative items complete the range.

- ***Stadtmitte,*** *Mauerstr. 9, Tel. (02 11) 9 89 45 00, www.elmartin.de*

Fromagerie
A cheese paradise, your dreams will come true and you may even try before you take your pick. Exotic ingredients, spices and an assortment of hams and salamis together with budget-priced wine: you will definitely come back.

- ***Unterbilk,*** *Neusser Str. 131,*
  Tel. (02 11) 3 98 36 82

Gewürzhaus Vogel
Locals are choosy when it comes to mustard. They preferably buy their mustard in this adorable, old fashioned shop with its smell of Oriental spices. Main speciality is A.B.B. mustard from Düsseldorf and of course many more sorts of mustard. Hundreds of different spices are on sale.

- ***Altstadt,*** *Mertensgasse 25,*
  Tel. (02 11) 32 57 88,
  www.gewuerzhaus.altstadt.de

Gut & Gerne
An assortment of plain chocolates you won't find in any supermarket. For example, there is a bar of chocolate that dissolves immediately in hot milk. A heavenly taste. Try it in the cosy café next door.

- ***Altstadt,*** *Burgplatz 3,*
  Tel. (02 11) 86 39 96 96
  www.schokoladenfachgeschaeft.de

La Maison de Bacchus
Budget-priced wine for everyday and top-class wine for special occasions; there is a wide choice in Bacchus' shop. You will be fascinated by the remarkable assortment of delicatessen like sauces Provencal or pates from the Pyrenees.

- ***Carlstadt,*** *Hohe Str. 48,*
  Tel. (02 11) 32 76 31

Linzbach
Linzbach is run by the family and convinced smokers praise the huge assortment of pipes and the biggest assortment of cigars in Düsseldorf. Highlights are two walk-in humidores for tobacco and cigars from all over the world.

- ***Stadtmitte,*** *Graf-Adolf-Str. 78,*
  Tel. (02 11) 36 23 02,
  www.tobacco.de

Nespresso
If you appreciate high quality, easy to prepare coffee and stylish capsule machines, visit the two-floors-Nespresso boutique on Königsallee. Excellent service and convenient purchasing procedure.

- ***Stadtmitte,*** *Königsallee 19,*
  Tel. (02 11) 0 80 01 81 84 44
  www.nestle.de

Pahlke
"Fish from Pahlke" locals answer when asked about their fish lunch. Pahlke has a stall on Carlsplatz and a shop in Gerresheim. There aren't many good fishmongers in Düsseldorf; you have to go to Gerresheim.

- ***Carlstadt,*** *Carlsplatz,*
  Tel. (02 11) 32 85 00
- ***Gerresheim,*** *Benderstr. 68,*
  Tel. (02 11) 28 71 92

Shochiku
You get your daily supply as if you were in Tokyo. Not only Japanese people buy there. Fresh sushi take-away with sauces, the

Öko-Markt Schadowplatz

complete Asian supermarket assortment, fresh fish and Japanese ceramics are on sale.

▮ ***Stadtmitte,*** *Immermannstr. 15,*
Tel. (02 11) 35 38 51
www.shochiku-online.com

Temma

The supermarket was chosen "Biomarket 2006". The assortment comes from regional farmers. About 8,000 articles are on sale: food, cosmetics and toiletries. There are a bakery and a bistro as well.

▮ ***Benrath,*** *Hauptstr. 47,*
Tel. (02 11) 71 26 39,
www.temma.de

JEWELLERY

Galerie Cebra

Gallery owner Anemone Tontsch presents jewellery made of most different materials and fabrics on 70 square metres. The shop is eye-catching; you just get everything, from silver rings with felt to the finest necklaces.

▮ ***Altstadt,*** *Andreasstr. 25,*
Tel. (02 11) 32 32 12,
www.galerie-cebra.de

Georg Hornemann

Master jeweller Hornemann creates unique items so incredibly beautiful that they are copied worldwide, though the copies never reach the original's beauty. Even if you can't buy for lack of money, it's worth having a look at the shining gold and the precious stones in the shop window.

▮ ***Stadtmitte,*** *Königsallee 46,*
Tel. (02 11) 32 00 68,
www.georg-hornemann.de

Globales Sein
Not far from the Kunsthalle and Art Academy a small shop full of Asian handicrafts and nice bits and pieces awaits customers. A smell of patchouli, a rich assortment of jewellery, clothes and interior décor are on sale.

- ***Altstadt,*** *Mühlengasse 10, Tel. (02 11) 13 13 62 , www.globalessein.de*

Karma Accessoires
Who thinks jewellery is for women only is proved wrong in Kapuzinergasse. Silver and dark black stones characterize jewellery made for men. Wallstraße offers jewellery for women who love kitsch.

- ***Altstadt,*** *Wallstr. 16, Tel. (02 11) 8 68 13 55,*

SOUVENIRS

Arthur Platz
Carnival, Easter, Halloween, Christmas or New Year: Arthur Platz is the top provider of fun articles in Düsseldorf. His small shop is an astonishing treasure trove and especially at carnival his costumes are fantastic.

- ***Altstadt,*** *Grabenstr. 1, Tel. (02 11) 13 24 24*

:D Düsseldorfer Senfladen
Museum and shop, it is a paradise for fans of the fine local Löwensenf (brand name) packed in little nostalgic ceramic pots. Information is provided about this really hot mustard and about cultivation and processing of the mustard plant.

- ***Altstadt,*** *Berger Str. 29, Tel. (02 11) 8 36 80 49, www.duesseldorfer-senfladen.de*

Et Kabüffke
The Busch family has been brewing these bitters made from around 100 spices, fruits and roots since the 19th century. The people of Düsseldorf consider it a type of medicine, so that people like to stop there for the last drink of the evening.

- ***Altstadt,*** *Flinger Str. 1, Tel. (02 11) 13 32 69, www.killepitsch.de*

Jeck' Jedöns
Owner Martin Wilms is a hard core carnival fan and proud of being the first to have established the first real carnival shop in Düsseldorf. Costumes for the fifth season are on sale all the year round. He features city guides and Düsseldorf accessories as well.

- ***Altstadt,*** *Marktstr. 6, Tel. (02 11) 86 32 42 80, www.jeck-jedoens.de*

Souvenirs – typical for Düsseldorf :D
There are a few local emblems and specialities that are eminently suited as small presents or souvenirs. The widest range of Düsseldorf souvenirs is available from the Tourist Information Offices.

- ***Altstadt (Old Town),*** *Marktstr./ corner Rheinstr., Tel. (02 11) 17 20 2-840*
- ***At central station,*** *Immermannstr. 65 b, Tel. (02 11) 17 20 2-844, www.visitduesseldorf.de*

Düsseldorfer Senfladen

Schadow Arkaden

SHOPPING GALLERIES

Düsseldorf Arcaden

This shopping centre with a size of 20,000 square metres opened in 2008 and offers a wide selection to suit every taste and budget.

▮ ***Unterbilk,*** *Friedrichstr. 133, Tel. (02 11) 31 11 06-6, www.duesseldorf-arcaden.de*

Kö-Bogen

The newest architectural shopping highlight by famous architect Daniel Libeskind combines exclusive fashion and accessory stores (Porsche, Windsor, Faber Castell, etc.) with trendy places to enjoy Italian meals or coffee. One half of the building is made up of Breuninger, a luxury fashion department store.

▮ ***Stadtmitte,*** *Königsallee 2, www.koebogen.info*

Kö-Galerie

Düsseldorf's first and very tasteful shopping mall is on the most elegant boulevard in town. 130 exclusive shops offer all the top brands on the market.

▮ ***Stadtmitte,*** *Königsallee 60, Tel. (02 11) 8 67 81-0, www.koegalerie.com*

Schadow Arkaden

A stone's throw away from the Kö, Schadow Arkaden is full of fashion wear. But the biggest shopping mall in town offers much more: furniture, food and the "Theater an der Kö" (theatre).

▮ ***Stadtmitte,*** *Schadowstr. 11, Tel. (02 11) 86 49 30, www.schadow-arkaden.de*

Sevens

This life-style gallery on the Kö was founded in 2000. There are seven floors to the gallery, hence the name. At lunchtime the ground floor is very busy; tasty food is served: German, Asian, Italian and Lebanese style.

▮ ***Stadtmitte,*** *Königsallee 56, Tel. (02 11) 8 63 27 60, www.sevens.de*

Stilwerk

A visit is worthwhile because of the elliptical architecture. 17,500 square metres and 45 shops on five floors offer top design in home furnishings: from accessories to complete furnishing concepts.

▮ ***Stadtmitte,*** *Grünstr. 15, Tel. (02 11) 86 22 81 00, www.stilwerk.de*

DÜSSELDORF
1 Königsallee
2 Stilwerk
3 Schadow Arkaden
4 Opera
5 K20
6 Kunsthalle
7 Heine-Haus
8 St. Lambertus
9 Schlossturm
10 Town hall
11 Schneider-Wibbel-Gasse
12 Carlsplatz
13 Maxkirche
14 Stadtmuseum
15 Racetrack
16 Meilenwerk
Torist-Information Office
Rheinwiesen
Oberkassel
Rhein
Rheinkniebrücke
Victoriaplatz
E.ON-Platz
Museum Kunstpalast
NRW-Forum Kultur u. Wirtschaft
Tonhalle
Joseph-Beuys-Ufer
Oederallee
Hofgarten
Hofgartenrampe
Tonhalle/Ehrenhof
Fritz-Roeber-Straße
Academy of Arts
Eiskellerstraße
Public Prosecutors Office
Ratinger Tor
Max.-Weyhe-Allee
Theater-museum
Scheibenstraße
Freiligrathstraße
Nordstr.
Kapellstraße
Duisburger Straße
Schäferstr.
Arnoldstraße
Inselstraße
Sternstraße
Pempelfort
Feldstraße
Rosenstraße
Kaiserstraße
Gartenstraße
Jägerhofstraße
Hofgartenstraße
Nördliche Düssel
Landskrone
Playhouse
Gustaf-Gründgens-Platz
Jan-Wellem-Platz
Hofgartenterrassen
Schadowplatz
Schadowstraße
Corneliusplatz
Elberfelder Straße
Deutsche Oper am Rhein
Heinrich-Heine-Allee
Th.-Körner-Straße
Blumenstraße
Martin-Luther-Platz
Königsstraße
Trinkausstr.
Heinrich-Heine-Platz
Ritterstraße
Ratinger Straße
Reuterkaserne
Altestadt
Liefergasse
Andreas-quartier
Paul-Klee-Platz
Grabbeplatz
Lambertus-Kirche
Lambertusstr.
Schlossturm
Town House
Hunsrückenstr.
Kurze Str.
Andreasstr.
Mertensgasse
Bolkerstraße
Town Hall
Markt-platz
Rathausufer
Rheinwerft
Altstadt
Rheinort
Rheinstraße
Flingerstraße
Alter Hafen
Akademiestr.
Wallstraße
Grabenstraße
Carlstadt
Schulstraße
Hetjens-Museum
Max platz
Carls-platz
Benrather Straße
Citadellstr.
Rheinufertunnel
Stadt-museum
Palais Wittgenstein
Heinrich-Heine-Institut
Bastionsstraße
Königsallee (Westseite)
Königsallee (Ostseite)
Stadtgraben
Josephinenstraße
Steinstr./Königsallee
Platz der Deutschen Einheit
Kreuzstr.
Stresemannstraße
Grünstraße
Berliner Allee
Alexanderstraße
Mannesmannufer
Berger Allee
Spee'scher Graben
Poststraße
Bilker Straße
Hohe Straße
Kasernenstraße
Breite Straße
Apollo Varieté
Carlstor
Südstraße
Schwanenmarkt
Karl-Theodor-Straße
Bahnstraße
Graf-Adolf-Platz
Graf-Adolf-Straße
Haroldstraße
North-Rhine Westphalian Parliament
Schwanenspiegel
Wasserstraße
Kaiserteich
K21
Ministry
Adersstraße
Studio Theater
Luisenstraße
Karl-Rudolf-Straße
Ernst-Reuter-Platz
Moselstraße
Neusser Straße
Reichsstraße
Elisabethstraße
Friedrichstraße
Talstraße
Lahnstraße
Corneliusstr.
Friedrichstadt
Police-Headquarters
Herzogstraße

Düsseldorf's heart beats in the Altstadt and Carlstadt, a few blocks away. **Carlstadt** is worth a visit if you are interested in antiques, art and second-hand bookshops. It is the centre of modern Düsseldorf. It was circumvallated by walls and ditches until 1802. The bastion was destroyed when Napoleon occupied the Rhineland. He had parks installed on the grounds of the bastion: Stadtgraben (today's Königsallee), Hofgarten, Ständehauspark and Spee'scher Graben.

Several processions and parades take place within the boundaries of the Altstadt every year: Rosenmontag (Monday before Ash Wednesday), Schützen (shooting club) round July 20th, Corpus Christi and Martinmas, November 10th, with lanterns. The parades and processions go all the way from St. Lambertus, Schlossturm, Rathaus, Brauerei-Gaststätte Uerige, Carlsplatz to Maxkirche.

The **Altstadt** stands for social life in numerous pubs, for shopping, for culture, for quiet living in Carlstadt with its many galleries, studios, museums and a puppet theatre.

TIPS

- **Altstadt:** Eating-out, shopping or cultural events, the historical centre is a must.
- **Carlsplatz:** A compelling market with intriguing offers and food for the meal in-between.
- **Königsallee:** The world famous boulevard is a synonym for luxury.
- **Schlossturm:** This tower is the last remains of the princely residence, the castle burned down in 1872.

Königsallee (1) is definitely a top sight of Düsseldorf. The **Kö** (that's what Düsseldorfers call it) is a synonym for fashion, luxury and shopping without limits. This world famous boulevard is a most trendy shopping mile for the rich and the beautiful, for stars and starlets. But above all it is an cat-walk event open all year, not only for professional models. People move along on the extra-wide pavement some know where they are bound for but many go to see and to be seen. When Düsseldorfers say: "I'll go down the Kö" they think of a multifunctional plan: maybe shopping, maybe having a snack or a champagne or a coffee or an ice-cream. At any rate they want to enjoy watching people of all colours and nationalities, well dressed, badly dressed, poor or rich.

Even Düsseldorf's oldest shopping gallery is at the Kö: The **Kö-Galerie** not only offers "shopping deluxe", good food is served as well.

Kö-Galerie, *Königsallee 60*

➲***page 95***

The **Stilwerk (2)** at Grünstraße, a street off the Kö, specializes in furnishing and accessories. The concept store was built on the ground of a former swimming pool in 2000. On five floors you'll find art galleries, offices and top design shops that sell high-quality furniture, kitchen furniture and lamps. The shops are construct-

Rhine water front with St. Lambertus and the Schlossturm

ed round a 32-metre-high central hall that is elliptically shaped and bathed in light.

Stilwerk, *Grünstr. 15* ➲page 95

Window-shopping makes you feel hungry. There are lots of places to go to. Try the highly frequented shopping gallery **Schadow Arkaden (3).** You'll find **Poccino** with Italian snacks like panini sandwiches and with a restaurant at the back. The food centre in the basement offers food for every taste. You choose and you meet at bar tables with stools in the middle of the room. Light enters through the dome.

Schadow Arkaden, *Schadowstr. 11* ➲page 95

On the whole, the **Altstadt** is one big attraction – that's what most Düsseldorfers think and people from the hinterland, too. They often go there in the evenings and at the weekends to enjoy themselves: to whoop it out, to have a good time, whatever the cost, have drinks, have a party. People from the Rhineland have loads of synonyms for what you can do in the Altstadt. It is often called the world's longest bar counter, but Düsseldorfers don't like this vulgar term and tend to smile wryly when they hear it, because the Altstadt is more than just a long bar even though there are more than 300 pubs, restaurants, bars and discos. Numbers change everyday, some move away, others move in. Big discos known all over Germany like Pferdestall and

Lord Nelson were legendary in the 60s and 70s. Stars and corporate moguls went there and easily paid 80 German Marks (roughly 40 euro today) for a bottle of vodka. They loved watching the extremely beautiful young girls dance. Cream Cheese was the place for the art elite from the neighbouring academy. Dr. Jazz offered ambitious music. Talented and unknown rock players performed in Em Pöötzke.

Institutions like the **Hausbrauereien** (breweries) haven't changed. Füchschen, Schumacher, Schlüssel and Uerige.

- ***Im Füchschen,*** *Ratinger Str. 28* ***➲page 57***
- ***Schumacher,*** *Im Goldenen Kessel, Bolkerstr. 44* ***➲page 57***
- ***Uerige,*** *Berger Str. 1* ***➲page 57***
- ***Zum Schlüssel,*** *Bolkerstr. 41–47* ***➲page 57***

Above all – and Düsseldorfers know it well – the Altstadt is not only disco or boutique or bar or Döner Kebab or funky or touristy. On the contrary, it is a small, very lively and a diverse area. You'll find museums and cultural institutes scattered all over: the **Opera (4), K20 (5), Kunsthalle (6)** at Grabbeplatz, the **Kom(m)ödchen** in the basement of the Kunsthalle and the **Heine-Haus (7).**

- ***Opera,*** *Heinrich-Heine-Allee 16a* ***➲page 27***
- ***K20,*** *Grabbeplatz 5* ***➲page 24***
- ***Kunsthalle,*** *Grabbeplatz 4* ***➲page 26***
- ***Kom(m)ödchen,*** *Kay-und-Lore-Lorentz-Platz* ***➲page 28***
- ***Heine-Haus,*** *Bolkerstr. 53* ***➲page 29***

The Heine-Haus is historically situated at the heart of the Altstadt. **Heinrich Heine** was born there in 1797. This remarkable poet was born in Düsseldorf.

But one tends to have problems with sons and one doesn't always treat them nicely. They are renitent, question their background, criticise, keep nagging and call a spade a spade. Düsseldorf has always been very ambiguous towards this great Jewish poet. His journey to Paris was no doubt a way out of the petit bourgeois world of Düsseldorf, out of the dreary atmosphere. (He died in Paris and was buried there.) They were just not capable of dealing with powerful freethinkers. The Austrian Empress Elisabeth experienced the same when she suggested putting up a monument for Heinrich Heine, whom she deeply respected: the Düsseldorfers refused. At the beginning of the 1980s the University was named after him after a long and difficult struggle.

Heinrich-Heine-Haus was opened on February 7, 2006, his 150th anniversary. **Müller & Böhm Literaturhandlung** (book shop) and an expensively renovated cultural hall are inside. Sunday morning matinees are popular and a Lesecafé invites the guests to stay.

- ***Müller & Böhm,*** *Bolkerstr. 53* ***➲page 29***

The absolute centre is **St. Lambertus (8).** The bent tower of the basilica is the result of a construction error after a fire in the steeple top. It has become Düsseldorf's promi-

TIPS

HopOn HopOff City Tour
The daily round trip is a Düsseldorf highlight - with eight stops for you to hop on, hop off, discover and experience! Two children may travel free of charge per adult. 1-day-ticket €15

Information & Tickets Düsseldorf Marketing & Tourismus GmbH
Tel. (02 11) 1 72 02-854
www.duesseldorf-tourismus.de/en/hopon

nent landmark. Inside the Gothic church you find many elaborate side altars and holy pictures. The walls round the high altar give an idea of the size of the original choir. Stiftsplatz between the church and the rectory is secluded and seems far away from the noisy and busy Rheinpromenade.

St. Lambertus, *Stiftsplatz 7*

➲page 31

Ratinger Straße used to be the most important connection from St. Lambertus to the eastern hinterland. Well-known pubs and breweries have moved into the old houses. The **Ratinger Tor** was built by architect Adolph von Vagedes in 1815 and is reminiscent of the old bastion that gave way to Hofgarten as well as today's Heinrich-Heine-Allee and Kö.

The grounds of St. Lambertus border on the **Düssel.** The last few metres of the river, where it flows underground into the Rhine, adjacently to the cellars of the **Schlossturm (9)** at Burgplatz, cannot be seen. This tower has been carefully restored because it is the last remains of the princely residence. The castle which burned down in 1872 was not rebuilt. The **SchifffahrtMuseum** (maritime museum) is in the tower and from the bistro right on top, called Laterne, you get a splendid view across the rooftops of the Altstadt and the Rheinuferpromenade. The spot where the Düssel goes subterranean is marked by the **Stadterhebungsmonument** (monument to the granting of "town" status). Sculptor Bert Gerresheim completed it in 1988 to commemorate Düsseldorf's 700th anniversary. Lots of symbols show how Düsseldorf was proclaimed town and received the town laws after the battle of Worringen in 1288.

SchifffahrtMuseum, *Burgplatz 30*

➲page 27

There are close connections between the baroque **Andreaskirche** at Andreasstraße and the castle. It belonged to the court and Jan Wellem is buried in the mausoleum. The church was built by Jesuits and, on the orders of the prince, they founded a Kolleg (college), today's Stadthaus (town house) at Mühlenstraße/Andreasstraße. The Lutheran **Bergerkirche** (with its modern interior) is difficult to find because it is in a courtyard on Bergerstraße. The reform church **Neanderkirche** at **Bolkerstraße** has one tower, which was a station for the city night watchman for a long time. It only became part of the skyline, because the two buildings which blocked the view were destroyed during WWII. The churchyard is the beer garden of the brewery **Schlüssel,** a good example of the typical interlacing of culture and leisure in the Altstadt.

The pleasure of shopping or leisure often overlays the traces of history to be found on buildings – for example on the former pub Zum Kurfürsten on **Flingerstraße** No. 36, or on the former Volkshaus der Arbeiterbewegung (house of the labour movement) on **Flingerstraße** No.11, built in 1909 by the architects Moritz/Stahl, or on the gable houses in Zollstraße. During post-war reconstruction, city planners tried to reproduce former types of brick facades using small sections. The **Schneider-Wibbel-Gasse (11)** is full of restaurants and a tourist attraction: a clock with chimes has been attached to the building in memory of Tailor Wibbel, a fictional character from a play, who cunningly avoided a prison sentence. The famous little tailor figure appears daily, at 11am, at 1pm, 3pm, 6pm and 9pm. Music accompanies his appearance.

Going back to the historical part, past pubs, speciality shops for coffee, chocolate and handicrafts to the market place. Heinrich Tußmann built the **town hall (10)** (Rathaus) in 1573. It is remarkable because of the Renaissance gable and the stair tower. The town council meets in the spectacular Jan-Wellem-Saal. It is a sort of home for Düsseldorfers where they often meet: at Martinmas the children sing there, the Schützenfest (marksmen's festival) champion greets his fans from the balcony and the mayor answers Hoppeditz at the beginning of Carnival (Hoppeditz is the carnival fool). The baroque town hall is part of a group of buildings from various periods: The former Kurfürstliche Galerie with a façade from the 1920s (at the corner of Burgplatz), the former art college (today **Galerie der Kunstakademie**), the **new Rathaus,** built in 1958 to replace the destroyed part and the façade of the old theatre.

Rathaus, *Marktplatz 2*

Rathaus

Jan Wellem at Marktplatz

Markets no longer take place in front of the town hall, they moved to **Carlsplatz (12),** only a few hundred metres away. The former farmers' market is very picturesque. It is one of the best known markets in Germany and it is open all year. Carlsplatz is to Düsseldorf what the Viktualienmarkt is to Munich. Prices are high but a visit is always worthwhile: beautifully decorated ranges of goods – exotic fruit and vegetables, poultry, fish, meat, flowers, cheese, bread, spices from far away. It is a meeting point for people who like good food and for the chef of well known restaurants, especially on Saturdays. They all hunt for specialities, have a talk with the merchants (they like it!) or just look around. If the weather is nice, you'll find the employees of the surrounding banks and shops having their lunch at one of the snack stalls. A soup at **Deuser's** or fish at **Pahlke's** is the usual thing but there are more exotic snacks on offer.

Carlsplatz connects Altstadt and Carlstadt. Prince Carl Theodor developed the town following the principles of the baroque, using a regular square raster for the streets. Along the streets you'll find prestigious mansions, for example along Bilker Straße: **Palais Wittgenstein** (No. 7 with hall and **Marionettentheater**), the **Heine-Institut** (No. 12 and 14), the **Wohnhaus von Clara und Robert Schumann** (No. 15). Many artists have their **studios** in the secluded court-yards.

Marionettentheater

Stadtmuseum

- ***Marionettentheater,*** *Bilker Str. 7* ➲*page 28*
- ***Palais Wittgenstein,*** *Bilker Str. 7–9* ➲*page 30*
- ***Heine-Institut,*** *Bilker Str. 12–14*

The former fortified **Zitadelle** (bastille) with the baroque church **St. Maximilian (13)** is the central point of Carlstadt. It is one of the three Catholic churches in the Altstadt, it was built by the Franciscans together with a monastery. The town house of the Catholic Church, the **Maxhaus,** is located there (Schulstraße 11). The citadel was probably built before Carlstadt, and Citadellstraße with its town houses (particulary marked is No. 8, home of the Polish Institute) accurately reflects the epoch. The old town walls can be traced at the bastions. **Palais Spee** is on **Bastion Spee** (Bäckerstraße/Berger Allee). It holds the **Stadtmuseum (14)** and architect Niklaus Fritschi succeeded in adding a harmonic new building.

- ***St. Maximilian,*** *Citadellstr. 2a* ➲*page 31*
- ***Stadtmuseum,*** *Berger Allee 2* ➲*page 24*

There are two highlights for horse-power fans: if you like horses you must visit the race course in Grafenberg; if you like old cars you must go to Meilenwerk.

The **racetrack (15)** on Grafenberg is a true gem. Düsseldorf riding club was founded in 1844 but the race course was only completed on May 15th, 1909. The course is said to be one of the most beautifully situated in Germany. Like Ascot, the horses run in a triangle first downhill and then uphill. After the Second World War, major races with high prizes were held in Düsseldorf.

- ***Racetrack,*** *Rennbahnstr. 20*

More horse power is promised at **Classic Remise (16),** a Classic Remise meeting point for those who have a special relationship with cars. Expensive vintage cars and car lovers' models from Golf I to VW bus are on offer, in best condition and in abundance. Interested parties can stroll around the Ringlokschuppen, a listed building, and buy or sell very special kinds of vehicles. There is even a garage where you can have your car restored or repaired. Not only millionaires hunting for a Mercedes SSK from the 30s go there, but also the man in the street.

- ***Classic Remise,*** *Harffstr. 110a*

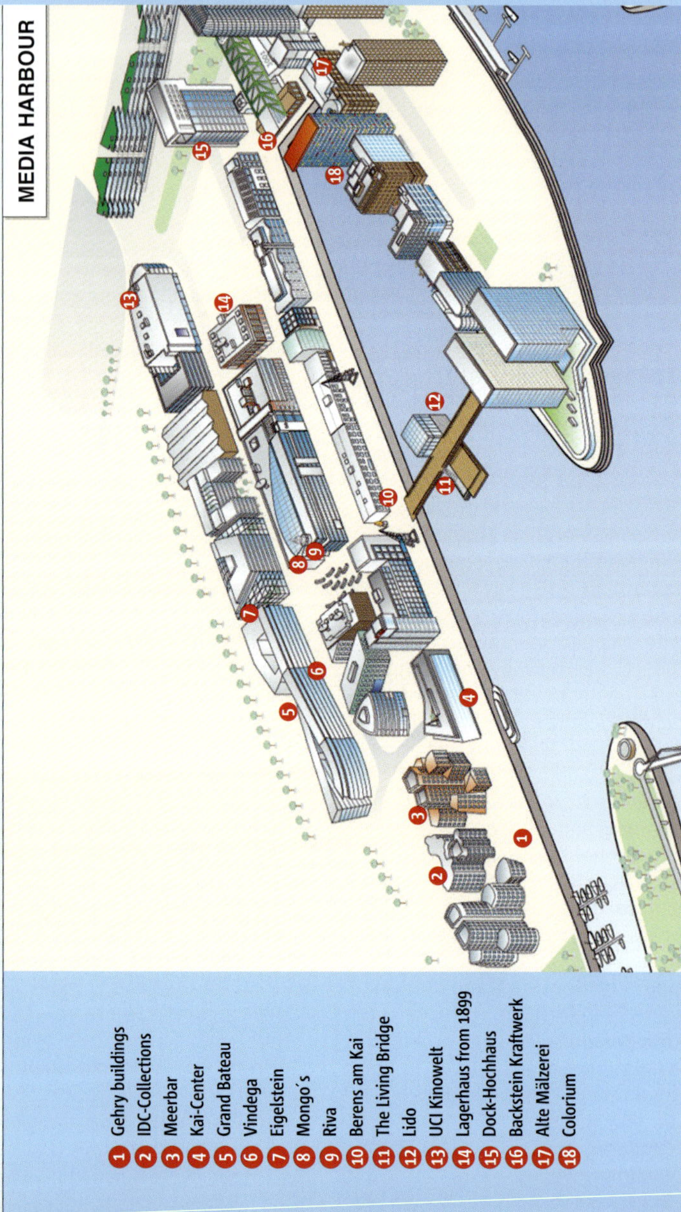
MEDIA HARBOUR
1 Gehry buildings
2 IDC-Collections
3 Meerbar
4 Kai-Center
5 Grand Bateau
6 Vindega
7 Eigelstein
8 Mongo´s
9 Riva
10 Berens am Kai
11 The Living Bridge
12 Lido
13 UCI Kinowelt
14 Lagerhaus from 1899
15 Dock-Hochhaus
16 Backstein Kraftwerk
17 Alte Mälzerei
18 Colorium

TIPS

- **Gehry buildings:** The three leaning office towers at the entrance of the media port are landmark and an attraction of modern Düsseldorf.
- **Kai-Center:** A ship-like building.
- **Meerbar**: The combination of bar, lounge and restaurant in the brick Gehry building is lavishly decorated and crowded at the weekends.

Düsseldorf is financially very well off. You can touch, feel and see its wealth in the new **Hafen** (port). In the 1980s this part of Düsseldorf was full of old cranes and shabby factory buildings. It smelt of granaries and corn mills. Cargo ships loaded and unloaded their goods. And then all became very quiet: a dying industry in a dying area. Slowly the Medienhafen developed; an architectural 'wonder' often copied and well-known Europe-wide. Many firms connected with media – radio, television, printing and computer – have their offices there, hence the name. But, in reality, this former port is much more; it is a melting pot of a new lifestyle culture that combines living, work and food.

Thousands of people work there and some live in the district - and they all feel like eating and drinking several times a day. An eating-out culture has developed, so far unknown in Düsseldorf. In the 1980s there were only a few corner pubs waiting for harbour workers. Today, top-class restaurants, original bistros, small bars and other gastronomic novelties wait for customers. You should find what you're looking for, even fried curry sausage with gold leaves.

Spotlight and landmark of modern Düsseldorf are the three leaning office towers by **Frank O. Gehry (1)** at the entrance to the Medienhafen. If the towers didn't have such normal-looking windows, one on top of the other in rank and file, the buildings would look like sculptures and not like buildings. That is exactly what the American top architect had in mind: he didn't want a high-rise building with special effects; he wanted a built piece of art with offices inside, appropriate for the district. And that's what he set out to achieve. After talking to the investors and to the city developers the basic idea was agreed on: three buildings with enough room in between for passages to the harbour basins.

Gehry buildings

The Old Port in the Altstadt

Gehry had a different approach – he wanted to create a sculpture as part of the district. The different fronts are well chosen, the tower with the bricks, close to the harbour picks up the brick fronts of the harbour buildings. The white walls of the other high tower correspond more to the houses along the Rheinuferpromenade (Rhine riverside road). The small tower inbetween the two high ones was sheathed in steel sheet and reflects the surroundings: the bricks, the white wall and of course, the sky. The steel sheets are slightly bent and not even. They distort the mirror images and produce unusual effects: not cold and hostile but very alive.

An architectural landscape with an interesting mixture of old and new buildings developed round the basin of the former industrial harbour. The old harbour and its water basins inspired the architects. Several buildings, like the **Kai-Center (4)** (Kaistr. 20) or the **Grand Bateau (5)** (Zollhof 2–8), look like ships. It's a special feeling watching an elegant cruiser entering the harbour – the Kai-Center (architects

The harbour at night

Döring, Dahmen, Joeressen) gives you exactly the same sublime feeling. It's amazing: the glass front looks as smooth as a steel hull. No window frames can be seen and you can't tell the difference between the windows that open and the immobile glass elements. There are no visible steel elements that support the construction. Technical innovations made it possible: special inner profiles were developed, which were fixed to the glass structure.

Instead of working in warehouses people work in offices, studios and ateliers. Typical warehouses were not pulled down but put under monumental protection. A few cranes were kept in memory of the old days. The new buildings are fascinating and attract many visitors. Some were hardly changed and others were elaborately restored like the **Lagerhaus** from 1899 **(14)** (Kaistr. 3). Its front with white walls, structured with brick base and brick linings is considered as an excellent example of industry architecture. The **Alte Mälzerei (17)** (Speditionsstr. 7, architect Gansfort) kept its beautiful front as did Lamer's silo and Lamer's villa (Speditionsstr. 13) or the **Backstein-Kraftwerk (16)** with its gates in red and white (Am Handelshafen 4). Many of the modern buildings interact with the old harbour architecture and change it. The combination of high-rise and one-storied buildings adds an exciting element to the skyline and is a modern addition to the Rhine front of Altstadt and Carlstadt.

Again the idea of a ship behind the construction: at the other end of Hammer Straße and Zollhof right before Franziusstraße the cinema **UCI Kinowelt (13)** (architect Till Sattler) looks like a round stern. However, it is not as closed as a ship stern; you can see the foyers in front of the nine auditoria

On the Living Bridge

Meerbar

and the restaurant through metal and glass elements.

Cranes inspired the architects when building **Dock-Hochhaus (15)** (Kaistr. 2, architect Coenen) and **Colorium (18)** (Speditionsstr. 9, architect Alsop). The roof overhangs like the mounting for cranes. Colorium is the only building with a colourful front, hence the name.

It's best to enjoy the Medienhafen on foot. The new **Living Bridge (11)** across the basin with the first class restaurant **Lido (12)** allows a round tour through the district.

It's now time to talk about eating-out and nightlife in the media harbour.

Not only the rich and beautiful - and those who would like to behave the Düsseldorf media harbour on their agenda. There is a lot to enjoy and even more to see in the bars and restaurants, even for "normal" people who just want to chill in cosy lounges. If you are in love, you'll enjoy the sunset from one of the terraces together with cocktails, pasta or seafood. Most spectacular is the glazed **Lido** on the new bridge across the harbour basin. The menu has a French touch with lots of seafood. In summer you can sit directly above the water. At Hammer Straße the **Eigelstein (7)** attracts trendy people with Kölsch (beer from Cologne). If you don't like it, have a Weizen (wheat beer) with Flammkuchen (onion quiche).

- ***Eigelstein**, Hammer Str. 17, Tel. (02 11) 6 02 74 77, Mon–Fri 11am–1am, Sat 10am–1am, Sun 10am–12am, www.eigelstein-duesseldorf.de*
- ***Lido,** Am Handelshafen 15, Tel. (02 11) 15 76 87 30, daily 12pm–1am, www.lido1960.de*

Not inexpensive and very popular; **La Donna Cannone** serves classic Italian food at its best in a cosy atmosphere with classic furnishing and an extremely friendly service.

Extremely elegant is the **Meerbar (3)** in the red brick Gehry building. The combination of bar, lounge and restaurant is lavishly decorated and really crowded at the weekends. You'll have to be patient if you want a drink or finger food but you won't mind, it is fun to watch the people.

- ***La Donna Cannone,*** *Hammer Str. 28, Tel. (02 11) 39 60 05, Tue–Fri 12pm –3pm and 6pm–11pm, Sat/Sun 6pm–11pm, www.ladonnacannone.de*
- ***Meerbar,*** *Neuer Zollhof 1, Tel. (02 11) 3 39 84 10, Sun–Thu 10am–1am, Fri/Sat 10am–3am, www.meerbar.de*

Restaurant and Lounge bar **Riva (9)** at Zollhof is a trendy meeting point with a better service. At the brick-built bar you'll find the beautiful in-people - several times a week with live piano music.

Mongo's (8) asks you to use your imagination. You choose the ingredients and the cook prepares your favourite dish for you even several times at all-you-can-eat-events.

- ***Mongo's,*** *Zollhof 10, Tel. (02 11) 4 40 72 70, Mon–Thu 12pm–12am, Fri/Sat 12pm–1am, Sun 11.30am-12pm, www.mongos.de*
- ***Riva,*** *Zollhof 11, Tel. (02 11) 2 09 50 50, daily 10am–3am, www.riva-duesseldorf.com*

One of the top restaurants in the media port is **Robert's Bistro,** it was the first restaurant and people had to, and still have to, queue to get in. Everybody goes there: businessmen, trendy and hip people. They all have to wait, you can't make reservations; it's Paul Meister's and Rolf Peters' policy, the way they took it over from founder Robert Hülsmann. Once you are inside, you meet people or you just enjoy the delicious food, fish soup, oysters or the divine tongue of veal with foie gras. Some customers come just for the potato salad.

- ***Robert's Bistro,*** *Wupperstr. 2*

➲***page 66***

Another top place is **Berens am Kai (10).** Holger Berens, native Westphalian, celebrates his cooking on a very high level; there is hardly anyone as creative and ingenuous. His futuristic-style restaurant has a somewhat cool atmosphere and overlooks the water. You can count on exceptional dishes: lemon sole ragout, lobster with broad beans, caramelized skate in honey, and calf's head with squid. He creates real symphonies and they are so good that you can easily live with the rather unfriendly service.

- ***Berens am Kai,*** *Kaistr. 16*

➲***page 69***

Düsseldorf is a fashion centre, but don't expect to be able to to shop for clothes in the media harbour. Even though the number of fashion labels located in this area is high, they are only showrooms displaying the new collections year round.

DÜSSELDORF
1 Stadttor
2 Rheinturm
3 Landtag
4 Ständehaus
5 GAP 15
6 Stahlhof
7 Wilhelm-Marx-Haus
8 Carsch-Haus
9 Galeria Kaufhof
10 Drei-Scheiben-Haus
11 Schauspielhaus
12 Tonhalle
13 NRW-Forum
14 Museum Kunst Palast
Torist-Information Office
Rheinwiesen
Oberkassel
Oberkassler Brücke
Rhein
Rheinkniebrücke
Victoriaplatz
E.ON-Platz
Museum Kunstpalast
NRW-Forum Kultur u. Wirtschaft
Tonhalle
Tonhalle/Ehrenhof
Hofgarten
Nordstr.
Pempel
Academy of Arts
Public Prosecutors Office
Ratinger Tor
Theater-museum
Landskrone
Playhouse
Gustaf-Gründgens-Platz
Jan-Wellem-Platz
Schadowplatz
Corneliusplatz
Deutsche Oper am Rhein
Andreas-quartier
Paul-Klee-Platz
Grabbeplatz
Lambertus-Kirche
Schlossturm
Town House
Town Hall
Markt-platz
Altstadt
Alter Hafen
Hetjens-Museum
Max-platz
Carls-platz
Carlstadt
Heinrich-Heine-Allee
Martin-Luther-Platz
Steinstr./Königsallee
Platz der Deutschen Einheit
Stadt-museum
Palais Wittgenstein
Heinrich-Heine-Institut
Spee'scher Graben
Schwanen-markt
Apollo Varieté
North-Rhine Westphalian Parliament
Schwanenspiegel
Kaiserteich
K21
Ministry
Studio-Theater
Graf-Adolf-Platz
Ernst-Reuter-Platz
Police-Headquarters
Friedrichstadt
Königsallee (Westseite)
Königsallee (Ostseite)
Stadtgraben
Bastionsstraße
Benrather Straße
Haroldstraße
Graf-Adolf-Straße
Reichsstraße
Herzogstraße
Elisabethstraße
Friedrichstraße
Breite Straße
Kasernenstraße
Berliner Allee
Bahnstraße
Grünstraße
Kaiserstraße
Hofgartenstraße
Joseph-Beuys-Ufer
Ratinger Straße
Bolkerstraße
Flingerstraße
Rheinstraße
Wallstraße
Trinkausstr.
Königsstraße
Blumenstraße
Schadowstraße
Elberfelder Straße
Th.-Körner-Straße
Poststraße
Berger Allee
Mannesmannufer
Moselstraße
Neusser Straße
Wasserstraße
Luisenstraße
Adersstraße
Talstraße
Lahnstraße
Corneliusstr.

TIPS

- **Rheinturm:** A fantastic view over Düsseldorf, there is no better.
- **Ständehaus:** A former parliament building and today a museum and a fancy bar.
- **Stadttor:** The new city-gate has the shape of a parallelogram and won several awards.
- **Wilhelm-Marx-Haus:** Germany's oldest multistorey office building right in the town centre.

Did you know that Düsseldorf has one of the oldest high-rise office buildings in Germany? Düsseldorfers were thinking high as early as the 1920s. Wilhelm-Marx-Haus was built 1922–24 by the architect Wilhelm Kreis and named after the Lord Mayor. The Rheinturm, with its 240.50 metres, dominates the Düsseldorf skyline. The highest office building is the ARAG-Hochhaus.

Let's start with the **Stadttor (1)** at the end of the Rheinpromenade. It is not circular but also of an unusual geometric form: a parallelogram. It is the seat of the NRW-president and was designed first by Jürgen Overdiek and Karl-Heinz Petzinka and continued by Petzinka and Thomas Pink. Its form is based on the ground plan of the district and its streets.

A massive high-rise building would have overwhelmed the elegant and transparent Landtag and Rheinturm, the architects decided on a transparent glass construction. They did so in the extreme: the outer enclosures are made of glass and the supporting framework is visible. The steel tubing emphasises edges and corners. To guarantee good insulation and a pleasant atmosphere the well known principle of double glazing was perfected: the two side wings, with 16 storeys and a height of 56 metres, were put under a huge glass cover and a glass house emerged. There are 1.40 metres between the two glass walls to let the air circulate. Thermal effects cause stale air to rise upwards and cold, fresh air to be drawn in through the ventilation flaps. Due to a variety of climate technologies (cooling ceiling, heat exchangers, district heating) energy consumption was reduced by 70 % compared to a conventional building. There is no air-conditioning and the huge windows can be opened.

Stadttor

Rheinturm

On the ground floor Antonio Tufaro pampers his guests. **Il Portone** specializes in seasonal food. Classic Italian carpaccio, antipasti or pasta are on offer as well as fish, meat or seasonal specialities; for all tastes and budgets.

- ***Stadttor,*** *Stadttor 1*
- ***Il Portone,*** *Stadttor 1, Tel. (02 11) 6 00 96 06, Mon–Fri 12am–2.30pm and 6pm–11pm, Sat from 6pm*

Let's proceed to the **Rheinturm (2)**, the outstanding symbol of the Düsseldorfer Rhine skyline. You'll find it at the edge of the southern city centre, at the entrance to the Medienhafen and next to the Landtag and the building of the Westdeutscher Rundfunk (radio station). The Rheinturm was built from 1979 to 1982 by H. Deilmann; there is a restaurant at 172.5 metres, it rotates hourly. For technical reasons it moves in one direction between noon and 5.30pm and in the other between 6.30pm and 1am. The rest of the time it stands still. While enjoying a splendid view of the city you can choose from an international menu. The restaurant Top 180 and the bistro Panorama offer excellent food and snacks, both have a glazed platform. The journey up is very exciting. If you want to enjoy New Year's Eve or Fun Fair big fireworks together with a luxurious meal you'll have to make your reservation well in advance.

The view of Düsseldorf is breathtaking: Medienhafen, Altstadt, Hofgarten, Königsallee and the Rhine with its bridges; on a clear day you can easily see Cologne and the Bergische Land.

Have a good look at the portholes; it's a worldwide unique system: 39 of the 62 illuminated portholes form a decimal clock; separated by air traffic control lights and distributed over 160 metres of the tower shaft. The portholes have twelve light-emitting diodes (LEDs) each, consisting of four red, four green and four blue LEDs. The changing combinations of colours produce different effects.

- ***Rheinturm,*** *Stromstr. 20*
- ***Günnewig Rheinturm Restaurants,*** *Stromstr. 20, Tel. (02 11) 86 32 00-0, www.guennewig.de*

Next to the Rheinturm you'll find the **Landtag (3).** This building with

Landtag

its typical and unmistakable circle buildings started it all off and the old harbour district was completely reconstructed.

City planners decided to fill the basin to have an easier approach to the Rhine. So the new area offered itself as a prestigious place for the new Landtag.

Parliamentary parties were well aware of the atmosphere in the 70s, a monumental and towering building would not have been appropriate. They wanted the plenary hall to be round to symbolize the discussion forum of the parliamentarians. The architects Eller, Moser, Walter and partner won the competition: their construction, a seemingly mathematical building with circles and intertwining semicircular wings came closest to what was wanted. The plenary hall (diameter 30 metres) is a sort of fixed star surrounded by circular halls for parliamentary party sessions. The connecting straits are for offices.

The construction was not easy; intertwining circles had never been built before. How to fix a window properly if there are no corners? A solution was found using fix points outside the building.

Landtag, *Platz des Landtags 1*

The **Ständehaus (4)** stands in a pretty park with a pond. In former times it was the home of the parliament. Today the museum for modern art invites you to a tour under the impressive glassdome.

K21 im Ständehaus, *Ständehaus 1, Tel. (02 11) 8 38 16 00, www.kunstsammlung.de*

The latest tower building in town is **Gap 15 (5)** named after its address: Graf-Adolf-Platz 15. It is a combination of a 90 m high-rise modern building and a five-stored flat, historical-looking building connected by a bridge and a glass roof. The buildings are hosts to several companies such as Ernst and Young and lawyers' offices. While the flat building commemorates the former telecommunications office on whose grounds it was built, the taller building consists of two joining ellipse shapes and is shea-

Gap 15

Carsch-Haus

thed by glass elements. It has gained fame because of its green veil twice in its lifetime since 2005: Parts of the glass windows fell down and required several months of reconstruction.

▮ ***Gap 15,*** *Graf-Adolf-Platz 15*

Stahlhof (6) on Breitestraße is known for its refined ground plan: a square to the street and an oval staircase. Bonatz designed it as an administration centre for the Eisen-und Stahlkonzern Stumm (steel and iron works) in 1922; he won the competition way ahead of Kreis and Behrens. Bonatz focused on the vertical lines with his striking windows with bars and made the main building look slimmer and higher (it is nearly as high as the Wilhelm-Marx-Haus). He used a trick which convinced the panel of judges: he omitted a large street front, the wings retreat into the yard and in front is a flatter, more horizontally structured gatehouse. This sensitive way of dealing with structures hasn't lost its appeal. The necessary restorations (architect HPP) didn't change the proportions. The two impressive staircases were kept and the spaces between the wings were modernised to serve as offices.

▮ ***Stahlhof,*** *Breitestr. 69*

A further landmark of Düsseldorf is **Wilhelm-Marx-Haus (7).** Architect professor Wilhelm Kreis, director of the Düsseldorf art college, caused a sensation in 1924. The building has 12 floors including the attic and with its intertwining arcs it made history as the first German high-rise office building.

In the courtyard the **Bazzar** is a must for coffee fans. Inside the shop high-class espresso machines are on sale and outside a

Drei-Scheiben-Haus

glass of water is served with your cappuccino. Salted almonds go as well with the exquisite coffees. There is just one cup size. Baguettes are freshly prepared.

- ***Wilhelm-Marx-Haus,***
  Heinrich-Heine-Allee 53
- ***Bazzar,***
  Heinrich-Heine-Allee 53 ***➲page 70***

Today's accepted principle of protecting historical monuments was less heeded in the 1970s and they were simply moved to fit into the cityscape. The **Carsch-Haus (8)** (architect Otto Engler) at Heinrich-Heine-Allee was completely removed by 23 metres to make more space above an underground junction. It was carefully dismantled and reconstructed true to original. To keep the harmony of the ensemble Carsch Haus, the historical store **Galeria Kaufhof (9)** (architect Joseph Maria Olbrich) and the Wilhelm-Marx-Haus and to avoid visual-dissonance, the west wing of the Wilhelm-Marx-Haus was extended and the front was copied in every detail. Such a reconstruction of a historical building is much more controversial today and would no longer be considered.

- ***Carsch-Haus,***
  Heinrich-Heine-Platz 1 ***➲page 82***
- ***Galeria Kaufhof,***
  Königsallee 1 ***➲page 82***

Significantly older but no less spectacular is the **Drei-Scheiben-Haus (10),** a former administration building of Thyssen-Krupp AG. The construction consists of three buildings arranged parallel to each other. The building by architects Hentrich and Petschnigg from 1957 to 1960 sets an example for multi-storey architecture in Germany and is under monumental protection.

- ***Drei-Scheiben-Haus,***
  August-Thyssen-Str. 1

Ehrenhof/Kunstpalast

Right next to it is the architecturally striking **Schauspielhaus (11)** (theatre). It was one of the last post-war theatre buildings by architect Bernhard Pfau. First plans began with a competition in 1959 and opinions were very divided. At the beginning of the 1950s the city council had started on the restorations of the old Operettenhaus (music hall) much against the advice of experts and it remained a temporary solution. Another ten years went by, and then, on January 16th 1970, the new theatre was inaugurated. And it was a scandal. Demonstrators protested about the opening ceremony: invited guests only, no tickets on sale. The protest was to criticise the traditional cultural institutions and their exclusivity, they asked for more democratic participation. The fact that there were no boxes or circles in the big auditorium was seen as a positive sign towards a more democratic understanding of culture and was welcomed by the new post-war society. The small auditorium served as an experimental stage with its flexible seating.

The small auditorium has been most successful. Modern theatre was no longer an experiment and audience's participation a done thing. The big auditorium with its huge dimensions on the other hand has had problems in fulfilling the contemporary acoustic and visual demands made of modern theatre.

Schauspielhaus,
Gustaf-Gründgens-Platz 1 ➲***page 29***

Düsseldorf has always been fond of modern architecture. In 1926 the exhibition "Gesundheitspflege, soziale Fürsorge und Leibesübungen" (health care, social care, sports) took place. People call it "Gesolei", quite a practical abbreviation. It was again Professor Kreis who designed the ensemble and thus created a new architectural focus north of Oberkasseler Brücke. It

Ehrenhof

Tonhalle

has become a cultural centre under the name of **Ehrenhof** and includes museums and the **Tonhalle (12).** It was the initiative of the Düsseldorfer architects, HPP, to build a new Tonhalle as part of the museums district and to replace the old Tonhalle at Tonhallenstraße which had been destroyed during the war, too. They could convince the city planners. The interior was completely gutted and a concert hall was installed. The domed roof and the foyer were renewed. Rehearsal and administration rooms are in the arcades and the big vault holds part of the glass collection donated to the city by Professor Helmut Hentrich, honorary citizen. You feel that museums are close by: Günter Uecker designed the ceiling in the foyer, hanging bars illuminated from outside produce intriguing light effects. 21 parabolic mirrors, a light object by Adolf Luther, adorn the top of the cupola. Light is made visible by being reflected in the mirrors and its simultaneously illumination.

The art museum also had to be adapted to modern standards. During reinforcement of the load-bearing structure, the rooms were divided up differently and a new floor was added that is illuminated by a sawtooth roof but without changing the protected exterior. The former Landesmuseum Volk und Wirtschaft (people and economy) was similarly gutted and the **NRW-Forum (13)** has its exhibitions there. When restoring the **Museum Kunst Palast (14),** however, only the front was kept. It was built in 1902; later it was given a new front by Wilhelm Kreis. Oswald M. Ungers designed a new museum and an administration centre for Veba (today E.on).

- ***Museum Kunspalast,*** *Ehrenhof 4–5* ➲***page 26***
- ***NRW-Forum,*** *Ehrenhof 2* ➲***page 26***
- ***Tonhalle,*** *Ehrenhof 1* ➲***page 30***

9

ANNE-SOPHIE MUTTER 8. MÄRZ

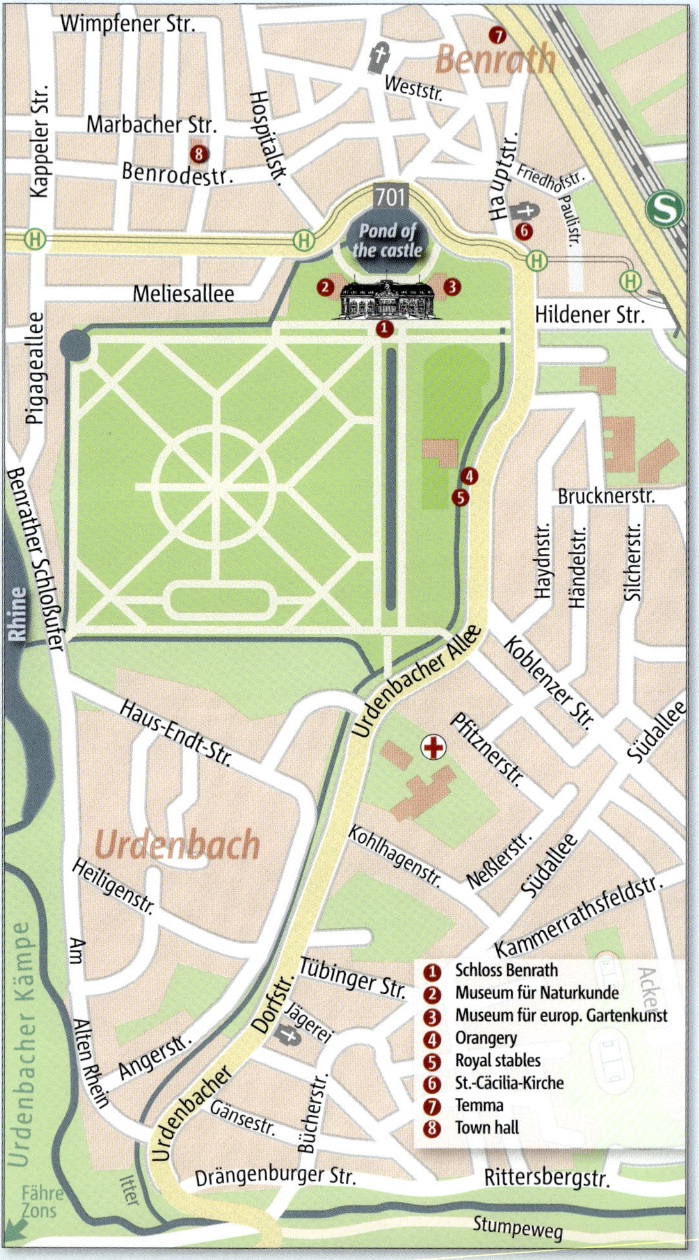
Wimpfener Str.
Benrath
Weststr.
Kappeler Str.
Marbacher Str.
Hospitalstr.
Benrodestr.
Hauptstr.
Friedhofstr.
Paulistr.
701
Pond of the castle
Meliesallee
Hildener Str.
Pigageallee
Bruecknerstr.
Benrather Schloßufer
Rhine
Haydnstr.
Händelstr.
Silcherstr.
Koblenzer Str.
Urdenbacher Allee
Haus-Endt-Str.
Pfitznerstr.
Südallee
Urdenbach
Kohlhagenstr.
Neßlerstr.
Heiligenstr.
Kammerrathsfeldstr.
Am Alten Rhein
Urdenbacher Kämpe
Tübinger Str.
Dorfstr.
Jägerei
Angerstr.
Urdenbacher
Gänsestr.
Bücherstr.
Drängenburger Str.
Rittersbergstr.
Itter
Fähre Zons
Stumpeweg
1 Schloss Benrath
2 Museum für Naturkunde
3 Museum für europ. Gartenkunst
4 Orangery
5 Royal stables
6 St.-Cäcilia-Kirche
7 Temma
8 Town hall

TIPS

- **Schloss Benrath:** The baroque summer residence is a cultural jewel of European standard.
- **Museums:** The wings house the museum of European garden art and the museum for natural science.
- **Castle garden:** Rich flowerbeds in front of the Orangery were designed for the Euroga in 2002.
- **Black Madonna:** The statue was consecrated in the Catholic church of St Cäcilia in 1677.

Benrath and its castle (1): a cultural jewel of European standard with the chance of becoming part of the World Cultural Heritage. The rural castle was built near the end of the baroque period and meant to be a summer residence, "Maison de Plaisance". Palace garden and castle are one work of art. The architecture and the division of rooms in the interior correspond to the construction of the garden. Prince Carl Theodor commissioned the castle, Nicolas de Pigage planned it and it was finished in 1773. Pigage's concept was to embed the castle into the garden. Stairs and terraces link the house to the garden.

The hall of mirrors in the castle corresponds to the mirror pond "Spiegelweiher" in the garden. The prince's and princess's private rooms in the side wings of the castle correspond to the small private gardens in front of the side wings. Public and private rooms alternate inside the castle and open garden spaces alternate with small intimate parts in the palace garden.

In former times the whole of the **castle garden** was surrounded by meadows and fields and the farms of Urdenbach and Benrath. It is divided in three large parts: the gardens of the 18th century round the castle; the western part, the "Boskett" (bosquet), and the eastern part with the Orangery and the gate building on Urdenbacher Allee, the last relicts of the original hunting lodge from the 17th century. The western and eastern parts are separated by the mirror pond. The northern part of the castle and the pond build the main axis of the castle garden.

A walk through the castle gardens gives you a good idea what garden culture was like in past centuries. If you are interested, information is available in the garden art museum in the newly decorated east wing of the castle. It was established in 2002 at the beginning of the European garden show (Euroga). In front of this wing you'll find the princess's private garden, the prime example of a classic French garden: abundant flowers in geometrical flowerbeds. Water gardens in the so-called triangles give a lively impression. The little river Itter enters the castle garden there and feeds all the waters of the palace garden.

On the opposite side, and next to the west wing of the castle, you'll find the former prince's garden. The subsequent castle owner, King Friedrich Wilhelm IV had the garden changed by Peter Josef Lenné in the mid 19th century. According to the taste of the time it became an English landscape-style garden.

After a stroll through the little private gardens you can enjoy the full architecture of the castle garden by walking along the mirror pond. Down the stairs from the terrace - in summer you have lovely pots there - you go through the sculpture garden, then cross the Fächerallee near the so-called "Bartschüssel" - a slope in the form of a razor bowl, hence the name. If you follow the the length of the pond you'll get to a vantage point called "Kurzweil" (pastime) and you'll have a good view over the Itter meadows, near-by Urdenbach and the quadrangular forest garden, the **Boskett.**

Bushes and trees on the edges of the Boskett seem to be a proper forest, but inside you can see the garden art. Two orthogonal axes cross the Boskett and their corners are especially formed. At the eastern side by the castle and the vantage point "Kurzweil", at the western side by the Rheinkopf (view of the Rhine) and the so-called Kopfweiher (head pond). The other corners of the orthogonal axes are formed by the riding arena with its beautifully shaped trees, a Lindenplatz (lime trees), a quadrangular pond and the trumpet pond next to the mirror pond. The area round the trumpet is like a room full of light, a fascinating play of light and shadow.

During Euroga 2002, a kitchen garden was reinstated to the east of the mirror pond on the basis of old plans and an abundant flower garden was made in front of the present-day **Orangery (4).** The buildings have thus been upgraded in accordance with their significance. The Orangery belongs to the old castle of Benrath. It was built as a hunting lodge in 1666 by Count Philipp Wilhelm. The former zoo was transformed into the Boskett by Pigage. Prince Carl Theodor had a new castle built, the old one was in ruins and a renovation would have been too costly. Only the fairly stable side wing was kept and used as Orangery.

Rulers have tended to build their stately homes in Benrath for good reason – it was always the location of a fortress or castle. The earliest owners were the von Benrode who had their ancestral seat there. In 1380 the von Bergs took it over and built a moated castle. It was destroyed during the Thirty Years' War. After that the hunting lodge was built and finally today's "Maison de Plaisance".

Over the centuries Benrath itself was a settlement that has drawn its importance from the neighbouring castle. Benrathers have always been proud of the castle and even today it's their 'parlour'. Many important events take place at the castle. At one point they even had a regatta on the mirror pond.

Schloss Benrath and its pond

The dedication of many initiatives, clubs and associations sped the restoration of the castle. Many cultural activities like concerts for example make the castle attractive.

A highly controversial example is the **Ensemble Modern Dance in the royal stables (Marstall) (5).** The critics are divided: some think the contemporary dance performances in the stables of Benrath castle by VA Wölfl and his group are a rather forced and muddled effort to produce art and the others see high intelligence and a world vision in their work. At any rate, the ensemble is touring successfully.

Benrath, *Marstall, Schloss Benrath, Urdenbacher Allee 10, Tel. (02 11) 7 18 77 77, www.neuertanz.com*

Apart from the ensemble there are three museums in the castle. The **Museum für europäische Gartenkunst (3)** is in the east wing. An exhibition on 2,000 square metres shows sculptures, paintings, graphics, china, rare books, models and media that represent themes and periods of garden art concentrating on the architectural style of "Maison de Plaisance". The visitor can explore the history of garden art, from antiquity until the present days in four tours. Main emphasis is put on the golden age between the 17th and 19th centuries.

The virtual tour of Düsseldorf and its gardens is something special: you get the villas and the "locus amoenus" of antiquity, Italian Renaissance, prestigious baroque gardens and English landscape-style palace gardens.

There are changing exhibitions on different themes of the history of gardens as well as on modern concepts. Public guided tours are every third Sunday at 2.30pm.

The museum **Corps de Logis** is the middle part of the "Maison de Plaisance". Regular guided tours show you how the "Maison de Plaisance" was used, how their owners fled the strict court ceremonies. Extra guided tours are on offer for those who want to know more about "The life of the servants", "Table manners at court" or "Hunting". The guided tours are more suitable for adults, but there are special events for children on how people lived and worked in former times.

The **Museum für Naturkunde (2)** in the west wing was founded in 1929. Lower Rhine area and Lower Bergisches Land are focused on: How the Rhine changed its course over the centuries, fishing, moorland, fenland, fauna and flora, trees in the castle garden and the Neandertal.

Worth mentioning is the **Benrather Vogeluhr** (birds' clock) with early-morning birdsong and an electronically simulated dawn as well as an observation bee hive with a bee dance clock. The exhibition offers a walk through the history of earth and mankind, "from the big bang to mankind". A small planetarium invites you to enter the world of stars. A "green classroom" gives pupils the chance to experience nature through their senses. In 2002 the museum started a collection that deals with regional environmental protection and nature conservation. The exhibition "Flüsse und ihre Auen unter besonderer Berücksichtigung des Rheins" (rivers and their meadows, especially the Rhine) show the rich variety of animals and plants in one of the richest biotopes in Europe.

Regular public guided tours every first Sunday at 11am

Benrath, *Benrather Schlossallee 100–106, Tel. (02 11) 8 99 71 40, Apr 1th–Oct 31st: Tue–Sun 10am–6pm Nov 1st–Mar 31st, Tue–Sun 11am–5pm, www.schloss-benrath.de*

At the castle

The lively pedestrian area surrounds the church of **St. Cäcilia (6),** first mentioned in the 13th century. It was part of the Neusser Quirinusstift and had a huge sphere of influence. The old church is no longer there: The modern new Gothic-style church (built by Wilhelm Sültenfuß) contains a Black Madonna, consecrated in

The park of Schloss Benrath

1677. The donor was Count Philipp Wilhelm on behalf of his wife Elisabeth Amalie. Since then Benrath has become a place of pilgrimage but less well-known and less famous than Kevelaer or Neviges. Nevertheless even today many Catholics come to worship the Black Madonna in the first week of October. They follow a tradition started by Philipp Wilhelm and his wife in 1677. Then it was a procession from Düsseldorf to Benrath. Today the event is celebrated with a procession of lights at the castle of Benrath every second Sunday in October. It is difficult to find historical traces in the centre of Benrath. They got lost in the development of the district in the 19th century when the administration centre and the **Town hall (9)** on Benrodestraße were built in neo-Renaissance style. The brick building of the Dankeskirche in Müllerstraße is also worth visiting.

The town centre with its pedestrian zone and the small streets conveys a friendly atmosphere: shops for everyday needs and many attractive boutiques.

Directly on the Hauptstraße is the organic supermarket **Temma (7)** , a shop which belongs to the Rewe-group. The assortment comes from regional farmers. About 8,000 articles are on sale; food, cosmetics and toiletries. There are a bakery and a bistro as well with changing daily snacks, fresh juices and desserts – if you feel hungry in between.
Benrath**, Hauptstr. 47* ***➲page 92

Worthwhile is a trip to neighbouring **Urdenbach:** village charm at its best; especially the Urdenbacher Dorfstraße with its well-kept half-timbered houses. The **Urdenbacher Kämpe** is a nature reserve near the Rhine. It floods when the Rhine overflows, so you won't find plants or animals there; but with its wild orchards, willows and alder trees it is a typical Lower Rhine landscape.

Meerbusch
Am Rheinblick
Kullenberg
Zur Rheinfähre
Langster Str.
Kierst
Am Rheindamm
Langst
Ferry
Kaiserswerth
An St. Swidbert
8
Ilvericher Str.
Am Oberbach
K9
Rhine
Düsseldorf
Niederrheinstr.
Fliednerstr.
Arnheimer Str.
Kaiserswerther Markt
Klemens-
platz
Schleifergasse
Rhine
Herbert-Eulenberg-Weg
An St. Swidbert
Fr.-von-Spee-Str.
Göresstr.
Am Ritterskamp
Burgallee
Barbarossawall
Kaiserswerth
Niederrheinstr.
Fährerweg
An St. Swidbert
Rheinbrohler Weg
Egbertstr.
Alte Landstr.
Kittelbachstr.
1 Stiftsplatz
2 Basilika St. Suitbertus
3 Kaiserpfalz
4 Galerie Burghof
5 Im Schiffchen

TIPS

- **Kaiserswerther Markt:** The old centre remains the focal point of today's borough.
- **Im Schiffchen:** Star chef Jean-Claude Bourgueil offers top-class food behind a historical brick façade.
- **Kaiserpfalz** (imperial palatinate): The beautifully situated historical ruin is used for concerts and theatre performances.
- **Basilika St. Suitbertus:** This important church is one of the most beautiful and clear style pillar basilicas of Roman period in the Lower Rhine area.

The old centre of **Kaiserswerth** can only be reached by crossing a bridge or the dike. At the **Stiftsplatz (1)** you'll find lots of historical buildings. On the east side you'll find the **Zehnthaus** (a place where farmers' tithes were kept: a "zehnt" or "tithe" means the tenth part of what they had) and the **gate tower** which marks the border of the abbey as independent area and with own jurisdiction (immunity). Nearby is a low building called **Beinhaus** because in former times the place was a cemetery and the dead were laid out there. Next door, through a gate with bars you'll reach one of the oldest preserved **Romanesque houses** in the Lower Rhine area. You can tell by the angularly stepped gable ends and the windows with centre column and arcs. The house was lived in by wealthy canons. Over the centuries it was rebuilt several times, neglecting the original concept. It was the work of many years to uncover the former layers, for example of the chimney place. Today it is used by the Catholic community and harbours the parish archive among others.

On the north side of the square, you'll find another equally important half-timbered house, the **Gimbornhaus** named after its builder. It is near the passage from Dauzenbergstraße to Kaiserswerther Markt and is said to be one of the first houses rebuilt after the destruction of 1702.

A pious legend says that **Friedrich Spee** was born in the house opposite with the wide entrance. The warden's son became a Jesuit priest and became known for his poetic songs and his condemnation

Stiftsplatz at St. Suitbertus

of witch trials. On the west side you have stylish buildings from the baroque period. Some have eight-ray stars, the symbol of St Suitbertus.

The **Basilika of St. Suitbertus (2)** is an important Romanesque church. Its classic interior with nave and transept from the 11th century makes it one of the most beautiful Romanesque pillar basilicas in the Lower Rhine area. Choir and porch from the 13th century are remarkable, too. The church has been carefully restored. The colours of the vault are historically authentic: professional restorers found particles of colour. The precious shrine with St. Suitbertus' bones is a remarkable piece of mediaeval craftsmanship.

Suitbertus built the first church at the beginning of the 8th century. Today's replacement seems rather modest because big towers are missing. It it said that the west portal did have a tower but it was pulled down in 1243 by the warden Gernandus because of war. Two west towers were built in the 19th century, but destroyed in the Second World War.

The **Kaiserpfalz (3),** the other centre of mediaeval Kaiserswerth, is only a few metres away from the abbey area. Emperor Friedrich Barbarossa's son Heinrich finished building the castle which his father Friedrich Barbarossa had initiated in 1174. Only a few ruins are left, but the wall with the big windows facing the Rhine and the long stairs show how impressive the castle must have been. Barbarossa had moved customs from Tiel to Kaiserswerth for political reasons. He chose the place because it had been a bastion for hundreds of years. Already in the 7th century a fortified Frankish court had been built there. It belonged to Pippin, the powerful Carolingian mayor of the palace. He gave parts of the property to the missionary and to bishop Suitbertus for a monastery. The Kaiserpfalz was extended later. Until 1016 German emperors stopped at the Kaiserspfalz of Duisburg when travelling through their empire. In 1050 emperor Heinrich III stayed in Kaiserswerth so there must have been a castle at that time.

The Kaiserpfalz has been continually threatened by complete decay. After the destruction in 1702 people used the stones to build their houses. Repeatedly people tried to save the ruins, Prussian conservator Paul Clement was one of the rescuers with historical awareness. In recent years a private initiative managed to secure the walls and save the image of the castle. Today the castle is colourfully illuminated at night and used for concerts and theatre performances.

A few steps from here you find the restaurant **Galerie Burghof (4).** The beer garden is a popular meeting point in summer – not only for Düsseldorfers. If you are lucky to get a seat on the wall you can have a drink and watch the sunset over the Rhine. Beer, non-alcoholic drinks, rustic beer garden food, budget-priced, are on offer. Priceless is the view of the Rhine.

Kaiserpfalz

Galerie Burghof, *Burgallee 1, Tel. (02 11) 40 14 23, www.galerie-burghof.de, daily 11am–1am*

The idyllic location at the dike has always been popular especially with artists. Dramatist Herbert Eulenberg lived in the first house at the dike called Freiheit (freedom). His villa became a meeting point for artists. The view from the southern edge of town towards the meadows is unspoilt; you can watch the boats on the Rhine and the **ferry** at the nearby quay that connects Kaiserswerth with the left banks. It is an important link between the two banks especially for biking tours.

There are two ways to go back from the oldest place of Kaiserswerth to the town centre with its market place. Both are interesting: along the Rhine or along the street **An St. Swidbert.** The street starts behind the gate of the ancient bastion on the old road to Düsseldorf. It is a narrow street with houses tightly packed and staggered, as is typical for old towns. The Capuchin monastery and the neighbouring old post office with an archway dominate on the left hand side. The monastery was founded in 1654, it was a hospice then and in 1679 it became a convent for Capuchins. The church was built in 1672 and contains a splendid baroque altar.

In the 19th century a Catholic girls' school moved in and the archiepiscopal Suitbertus-Gymnasium (High school) is still there today. The most splendid house is number 32; it was restored by canonist Maes in 1714/1715 as you can see from a chronogram. Along the opposite

River Rhine at Kaiserswerth

lane, through the abbey tower gate you'll reach the abbey church.

The street at St Swidbert ends at Kaiserswerther Markt directly next to the middle island with its double row of chestnut trees. The market was the secular and economic centre of the town. Until the destruction of Kaiserswerth the **Rathaus** was on that middle island and divided the market place in two. Later it moved to Kaiserswerther Markt 23 and today the district administration has its seat there. The western part of the market towards the Rhine at the dike gate, among the trees has always been busiest. Skippers had to stop their journey and pay customs duty at customs (house number 4). The customs officer sat in the watch tower, watched the boats and called them in to pay their customs. If a captain tried to get away without paying cannon gunfire rumbled unmistakably.

As in the olden days, hospitality is still going strong: many restaurants –from bistros to sushi restaurants – have been established round the market place. During summer you can sit on the terraces under the chestnut trees. There is a special treat for gourmets. Behind a historical brick façade you'll find **Im Schiffchen (5)** with one of the best known and most talented chefs in town: star chef Jean-Claude Bourgueil. You can watch him at work which is quite unusual in his class. The cooking genius has mainly given up traditional cooking and is concentrating on French haute cuisine. He owns a well-stocked wine cellar and the staff is attentive and as well-trained as you would expect from a high-class and highly priced restaurant. The restaurant **Enzo im Schiffchen** is more easy-going, but its food belongs also to the championsleague.

Restaurant Enzo im Schiffchen,
Kaiserswerther Markt 9 ***➲page 69***

North of the Kaiserswerther Market you'll find many lanes. One, the Mühlenturm leads directly to a former windmill at the edge of the old town wall, only the round base remains. At the mill starts Fliednerstraße that goes past the Lutheran church, a plain, classical building. The Lutheran community was small and poor but achieved worldwide popularity because of its minister **Theodor Fliedner** who came to Kaiserswerth in 1822. Together with his wife he founded a nursing home that later became the base of our modern hospitals and became known worldwide under the name of Kaiserswerther Diakonie (clerical welfare and social work).

Kaiserswerther Markt and the area round Klemensplatz are attractive for fashion fans. They'll find unusual things, modestly priced. "Nordik" is worthwhile visiting: make your Scandinavian dreams come true. In the heart of Kaiserswerth you'll find the right accessories to remember your holidays, nice bric-a-brac as well as exclusive items for the fine table, china from traditional Royal Copenhagen or luxery-brand cutlery from Georg Jensen.

Kaiserswerther Markt 5,
Tel. (02 11) 4 08 04 11

Off the beaten track in the nice Alt-Kaiserswerther Gutshof (manor) is **Interform Designmagazin**. A definite must for design addicts. You name it and Ina and Wolfgang Gärtner have got it: attractive, original and useful things produced by prestigious designers. Many are classified with the red dot of the Essener Design Forum NRW.

Arnheimer Str. 20, Tel. (02 11)
4 05 00 00, www.interform.de

Düsseldorf Marketing & Tourismus
offers, a two-hour-guided tour
through historical Kaiserswerth.
Info at www.visitduesseldorf.de
or Tel. (02 11) 1 72 02-854

St. Suitbertus in Kaiserswerth

GENERAL INFOS

Hello, Good afternoon | *Guten Tag*
Good evening | *Guten Abend*
Good night | *Gute Nacht*
Good bye | *Auf Wiedersehen*
please/thank you | *Bitte/Danke*
yes, no | *ja/nein*
right/left | *rechts/links*
straight on | *geradeaus*
good-well/bad-badly | *gut/schlecht*
free/occupied | *frei/besetzt*
open/closed | *Geöffnet geschlossen*
How are you? | *Wie geht es Ihnen?*
Beg your pardon | *Entschuldigen Sie!*
I don't understand you | *Ich verstehe nicht*
I don't speak German | *Ich spreche kein deutsch*
Do you speak English? | *Sprechen Sie englisch?*
How much is it? | *Wieviel kostet das?*
Where is...? | *Wo ist ...?*
What time is it? | *Wie spät ist es?*

DAYS AND TIME

Monday | *Montag*
Tuesday | *Dienstag*
Wednesday | *Mittwoch*
Thursday | *Donnerstag*
Friday | *Freitag*
Saturday | *Samstag*
Sunday | *Sonntag*
morning | *Morgen*
noon | *Mittag*
afternoon | *Nachmittag*
evening | *Abend*
night | *Nacht*
yesterday | *gestern*
today | *heute*
tomorrow | *morgen*
Apart from | *außer*
working day | *Werktag*
holiday | *Feiertag*
day | *Tag*
week | *Woche*

NUMBERS

zero | *null*
one | *eins*
two | *zwei*
three | *drei*
four | *vier*
five | *fünf*
six | *sechs*
seven | *sieben*
eight | *acht*
nine | *neun*
ten | *zehn*
fifty | *fünfzig*
one hundred | *einhundert*
one thousand | *eintausend*

LODGING

youth hostel | *Jugendherberge*
hotel | *Hotel*
single/double room | *Einzel-/Doppelzimmer*
with breakfast | *Mit Frühstück*
half-board | *Halbpension*
full board | Vollpension
night | *Übernachtung*
room available | *Zimmer frei*

FOOD

restaurant | *Restaurant*
café | *Café*
pub | *Kneipe*
menu | *Speisekarte*
I want to book a table for ... persons | *Ich möchte einen Tisch für ... Personen reservieren*
The bill, please | *Die Rechnung bitte*
vegetarian | *vegetarisch*

ON THE ROAD

airport | *Flughafen*
plane | *Flugzeug*
station | *Bahnhof*
train | *Zug*
bus | *Bus*
tram | *Straßenbahn*
stop | *Haltestelle*
ticket | *Fahrkarte*
departure | *Abfahrt*
arrival | *Ankunft*
harbour | *Hafen*
taxi | *Taxi*
car | *Auto*
rented car | *Mietwagen*
breakdown service | *Pannenhilfe*

IN TOWN

police | *Polizei*
town hall | *Rathaus*
lost property office | *Fundbüro*
embassy | *Botschaft*
post office | *Post*
stamp | *Briefmarke*
telephone card | *Telefonkarte*
church | *Kirche*
cemetery | *Friedhof*
museum | *Museum*
opera | *Oper*
theatre | *Schauspielhaus*
castle | *Schloss*
castle tower | *Schlossturm*
theatre | *Theater*
old town | *Altstadt*

EMERGENCY

hospital | *Krankenhaus*
Where is the next pharmacy? | *Wo ist die nächste Apotheke?*
doctor | *Arzt*
dentist | *Zahnarzt*
I've got a toothache | *Ich habe Zahnschmerzen*
I've got a stomach ache | *Ich habe Bauchschmerzen*
I'm allergic to ... | *Ich bin allergisch gegen ...*
I'm feeling sick | *Mir ist übel*
pacemaker | *Herzschrittmacher*

GENERAL

- The currency is the euro (€) like elsewhere in the European Union. Next to the US dollar the euro is the most important currency within the world currency system. One euro is 100 Cents. There are coins for 1, 2, 5, 10, 20 and 50 cent as well as 1 and 2 euro. While the front of the coins is the same in all countries, you'll find a national motive on the back. The bank notes are the same in all countries: 5, 10, 20, 50, 100, 200 as well as 500-euro notes.
- Generally banks are open Mon–Fri 9am–4pm, Thurs till 6pm.

WHAT ARE THE PRICES LIKE IN DÜSSELDORF?

Mineral water	2.30 €
Beer	1.80 €
Coffee	2.40 €
Caipirinha	7.50 €
Pretzel (Brezel)	1,10 €
Fried sausage (Bratwurst)	2.50 €
Roll with minced meat (Mettbrötchen)	2.90 €
Pea soup (Erbsenssuppe)	3.50 €
Pizza margaritha	4.50 €
French fries (Pommes frites)	2.10 €
Blood sausage with bread (Flönz mit Brot)	4.50 €
Knuckle of pork (Schweinshaxe)	13.50 €
Traditional marinated beef (Rheinischer Sauerbraten)	13.90 €
Traditional dish with potato, blood sausage, fried sausage, onions (Himmel und Erde)	9.30 €
Steak with mustard (Senfrostbraten)	16.90 €
Potato pancake (Pillekuchen)	9.00 €
Sushi	7.00 €
Waffle	1.70 €
Truffles with champagne	6.50 €
One piece of cake	3.00 €
One scoop of ice cream	1.00 €

- **Smoking:** *Be aware that smoking is prohibited in public buildings, airport and public transport, and also in pubs and restaurants. Besides it is forbidden to drop cigarette ends on the street.*

IMPRINT

Editing
Verena Bretz (Culture); Michael Brockerhoff (Leisure/On the road/Düsseldorf parks); Gian-Paolo W. Costa (Leisure/Sports); Stefani Geilhausen (Gastronomy); Cordula Hupfer (Shopping); Bernd Jolitz (Leisure/Sports); Hans Onkelbach (Welcome); Natascha Plankermann (Culture); Sylvia Rollmann (Leisure/ On the road, Wellness); Jessica Schwarzer (Gastronomy/Bars and pubs, Clubs); Birgit Wanninger (Gastronomy); Tigo Zeyen (Culture); update 4th edition Stefanie Buss

Picture credits
Bädergesellschaft Düsseldorf mbH: S. 51; Andreas Bretz: S. 18, 89, 115; Thomas Bußkamp: S. 10, 46; Düsseldorf Congress Veranstaltungsgesellschaft mbH: S. 42; Düsseldorfer Marionettentheater: S. 28; Werner Gabriel: S. 24, 40, 48; Uli Gerritzen: S. 1, 2, 20, 43, 94, 100, 103, 104, 105, 107, 108 (bottom), 109, 113, 116, 117, 125, 126; Kukilies & Kollegen GmbH: S. 33; Messe Düsseldorf GmbH: S. 9; Michael Rennertz: S. 3, 5, 6, 16, 22, 25, 29, 30, 34, 48, 49, 52, 54, 60, 66, 71, 74, 76, 95, 96, 108 (top), 114, 115, 119 (left), 120, 132, 133, 134; Museum Kunstpalast, Harald Reusmann: S. 118; RP-Archiv: S. 4, 8; Arkadius Zagrabski: S. 27, 36, 110, 119 (right), 127, 129, 131; all other pictures: Droste Verlag

Design: Droste Verlag
Cartography: Holger Grobusch
Printing and Binding: Werbedruck GmbH Horst Schreckhase, Spangenberg
ISBN 978-3-7700-1562-7
www.drosteverlag.de

BY AIR

Düsseldorf airport (the third largest in Germany) is ideally situated: the fair exhibition centre is a 3-minute-taxi-ride away, the city centre is about ten minutes away. A fast automatic sky train connects the terminals with the train station "Düsseldorf Flughafen", offering good traffic links. 300 trains stop daily: ICE, IC, EC trains, local trains and fast-commuter trains (S-Bahn).

- ***www.dus.com***

BY CAR

Düsseldorf is in the middle of the densest European motorway network: A3, A44, A46, A52, A57, A59

- ***www.autobahn.nrw.de*** *inform you about the current road situation and gives a forecast of the traffic situation within the following 60 minutes and how to avoid a traffic jam.*

BY TRAIN

Düsseldorf main station is on the busiest railway line in Germany. Outside the entrance on Konrad-Adenauer-Platz you'll find tram and bus connections and inside the building the underground to the city centre/ Oberkassel/ Kaiserswerth und Messe. All districts can be reached via underground or fast-commuter train (S-Bahn). The central stop in the city centre is Heinrich-Heine-Allee.

- ***www.bahn.de***

BICYCLE HIRE

- ***next bike:*** *register, find a bike at a place near you, enter a code and return it after use. www.nextbike.de*
- ***Radstation****: Rent a bike at Hauptbahnhof, Mo–Fr 7am–9pm, Sat/Sun 10am–8pm, Willy-Becker-Allee 8a Tel. (02 11) 5 14 47 11 or at Apollo-Platz: Apr 1st–Oct 31st Mo–Fr 12am–8pm, Sat/Sun 10am–8pm, Tel. (01 60) 98 15 09 12 www.radstation-duesseldorf.de*

PUBLIC TRANSPORT

In the area of the regional integrated public transport system Verkehrsverbund Rhein-Ruhr (VRR) you can use and change local and regional trains, metro, tramways and buses freely with your ticket.

The fare system inside the VRR:

- A short-distance ticket (Kurzstrecke) can be used for short trips up to 3 stops.
- The fare level (Preisstufe) A 1 is valid for all trips inside the boundaries of Düsseldorf.
- If you want to go to other cities, you have to choose fare level B, C or D, as indicated in the fare tables at stops.

Regional day tickets, especially if you want to pass over the VRR boundaries, e.g. to Cologne:

- SchönesWochenende (Nice Weekend) = DayTicket for up to 5 persons on a Saturday or a Sunday, valid throughout Germany, but only on local and regional trains (RB, RE, S), not on Intercity trains (EC, IC, ICE), but also on all trams, subways and busses.
- SchönerTagTicket (Nice Day), Mo–Fr from 9 am, Sat/Sun without restriction, DayTicket for up to 5 persons, valid in the whole state of North Rhine-Westphalia (e.g. to Cologne), in regional trains only (RB, RE, S) and all trams, subways and busses. There is a budget version for 1 person: SchönerTagTicket Single.

Some important ticket types in the VRR:

- Einzelticket = Single-trip-ticket
- 4er-Ticket = 4-trip-ticket (trips in succession or parallel for several persons)
- Tagesticket = DayTicket (valid for one person till shut-down)
- Gruppenticket = GroupTicket (valid for up to five persons until shut-down)
- HotelTicket = Some hotels offer a special service: a HotelTicket that is valid on all means of local public transport for the time you stay in the hotel.
- For many events, e.g. trade fairs, cultural and sport events, there are "KombiTickets", i.e. the admission ticket for the event is valid as a train/bus-ticket to and from the event.

Tickets have to be stamped before or at the first boarding (but not when changing the train or, in case of day tickets, when boarding again later). You get your ticket at railway stations, service centres, certain shops, at main stops (vending machines) or in U-Bahn-cars and trams (vending machines) and busses (driver).

The following types of trains and buses can be used with your VRR-ticket without extra charge (provided you paid the correct fare stage and the destination is within VRR boundaries, of course):

- RE = RegionalExpress = Regional Express Train (between city centres)
- RB = RegionalBahn = other local trains
- S = S-Bahn = suburban rapid train
- U = U-Stadtbahn = Light rail transit (or Express tramway, partly underground)
- Tramways in Düsseldorf and to some nearby cities (Duisburg, Krefeld, Neuss, Ratingen)
- SB = SchnellBus = ExpressBus
- Bus = local and regional buses

- ***Rheinbahn:*** *Tel. (0 18 03) 50 40 30, www.rheinbahn.de*
- ***VRR:*** *Tel. (0 18 03) 50 40 34, www.vrr.de*
- ***www.nahverkehr.nrw.de:*** *All important information concerning transport by bus or train*
- ***www.mobil-in-d.de:*** *Information on transport and mobility around Düsseldorf*

DüsseldorfCard

DüsseldorfCard includes free travel on buses and trains in the city area, free entrance to museums, reduced tickets to public guided tours of Düsseldorf, boat tours, opera, theatre and variety. (see fold-out page)

- ***Rates****: Single 1-day ticket €9, 2-day ticket €14, 3-day ticket €19; Groups (3 adults) or families (2 adults and max. 2 children under 14): 1-day ticket €18, 2-day ticket €28, 3-day ticket €38*

SHIPPING ON THE RHINE

KD – Köln Düsseldorfer

- *Tickets directly on the quay or: Tel. (02 11) 3 23 92 63 , www.k-d.com*

TAXI €1,70 (base fare €4,50, per kilometre €2,20)

- **For Disabled:** Tel. (02 11) 69 93 15 90
- **Rhein-Taxi:** Tel. (02 11) 21 21 21
- **Taxi-Düsseldorf eG:** Tel. (02 11) 3 33 33 or 9 99 99

POLICE
Tel. 110
Headquarters Düsseldorf,
Jürgensplatz 5–7,
Tel. (02 11) 87 00

AMBULANCE
Tel. 112

FIRE BRIGADE
Tel. 112

MEDICAL EMERGENCY
Info at Tel. (01 80) 5 04 41 00

DENTISTS EMERGENCY TREATMENT
Info at Tel. (01 80) 5 98 67 00

INTOXICATION EMERGENCY
Tel. (02 28) 1 92 40

EMERGENCY SERVICE PHARMACIES
www.aponodie.de

OPERATOR SERVICES
Domestic directory assistance:
Tel. 11 8 33
Overseas directory assistance:
Tel. 11 8 34

AIRPORT LOST LUGGAGE
www.dus.com

LOST PROPERTY
Erkrather Str. 1–3,
Tel. (02 11) 89 91,
www.duesseldorf.de

LOST CREDIT CARD
Tel. 116 116

AUTOMOBILE CLUBS
ADAC: Service-Center, Höherweg 101,
Tel. (0 18 05) 10 11 12

CAR RENTAL
Avis: Flughafenstr., Tel. (02 11) 4 21 67 47/48; Berliner Allee 26, Tel. (02 11) 8 65 62 20, www.avis.de
Sixt: Willi-Becker-Allee 10 Tel. (02 11) 7 20 02-0; Albertstr. 31, Tel. (02 11) 2 40 62 00; Flughafen Terminal Ring 1, Tel. (0 18 05) 26 25 25, www.sixt.de
Europcar: Konrad-Adenauer-Platz 11, Tel. (02 11) 1 73 81-0; Flughafen Ankunft/Arrival B, Tel. (02 11) 94 23 80, www.europcar.de
Hertz: Immermannstr. 65, Tel. (02 11) 35 70 25; Flughafen, Ankunftsebene (Arrivals floor), Tel. (02 11) 41 10 83, www.hertz.de

BABYSITTING SERVICE
K.I.N.D., Kalkumer Str. 85,
Tel. (02 11) 4 79 17 17,
www.kind-duesseldorf.de

DISABLED TRAVELLERS
Willi-Becker-Allee 6–8, Tel. (02 11) 89-96468, -96656

HOTELS * * * * *
Breidenbacher Hof
Königsallee 11, Tel. (02 11) 16 09 00, www.breidenbacherhofcapella.de
Hilton Düsseldorf
Georg-Glock-Str. 20, Tel. (02 11) 4 37 70, www.hilton.de/duesseldorf
Hyatt Regency Düsseldorfl
Speditionsstraße 19,
Tel. (02 11) 91 34 12 34
www.duesseldorf.regency.hyatt.com
InterContinental Düsseldorf
Königsallee 59, Tel. (02 11) 8 28 50, www.ichotelsgroup.com
Renaissance Düsseldorf-Hotel
Nördlicher Zubringer 6, Tel. (02 11) 6 21 60, www.mariott.de
Steigenberger Parkhotel
Königsallee 1a, Tel. (02 11) 1 38 10 , www.duesseldorf.steigenberger.de

Villa Viktoria-Hotel Garni
Blumenthalstr. 12, Tel. (02 11) 46 90 00, www.villaviktoria.com

HOTELS* * * *

ArabellaSheraton Airport Hotel im Flughafen Düsseldorf, Flughafenstr., Tel. (02 11) 4 17 30, www.sheratonduesseldorfairport.de
Ashley's Garden
Karl-Kleppe-Str. 20, Tel. (02 11) 5 16 17 10, www.ashleysgarden.de
Best Western Hotel Savoy
Oststr. 128, Tel. (02 11) 38 83 80, www.savoy.bestwestern.de
Courtyard by Marriott
Am Seestern 16, Tel. (02 11) 59 59 59, www.courtyard.de
Courtyard by Marriott Düsseldorf Hafen
Speditionstr. 11, Tel. (02 11) 4 93 90, www.courtyard.de
Dorint Hotel am Rosengarten Neuss
Selikumer Str. 25, Tel. (0 21 31) 26 20, www.dorint.de/neuss
Günnewig Hotel Esplanade
Fürstenplatz 17, Tel. (02 11) 38 68 50, www.guennewig.de
Holiday Inn Düsseldorf
City Centre-Königsallee, Graf-Adolf-Platz 8–10, Tel. (02 11) 3 84 80, www.holiday-inn.com/dus-cityctr
Holiday Inn Düsseldorf-Neuss
Anton-Kux-Str. 1, Tel. (0 21 31) 18 40, www.holiday-inn-hotel.de
Hotel Nikko
Immermannstr. 41, Tel. (02 11) 83 40, www.nikko-hotel.de
Innside Residence-Hotel Düsseldorf/Ratingen
Am Schimmersfeld 9, Tel. (02 11) 42 70, www.innside.de
Innside Residence-Hotel Düsseldorf-Seestern
Niederkasseler Lohweg 18a, Tel. (02 11) 52 29 90, www.innside.de
Lindner Congress Hotel Düsseldorf
Emanuel-Leutze-Str. 17, Tel. (02 11) 5 99 70, www.lindner.de
Madison Hotel I
Graf-Adolf-Str. 94, Tel. (02 11) 1 68 50, www.madison-hotels.de
Melia Düsseldorf
Inselstr. 2 Tel. (02 11) 52 28 40, www.melia.com
Radisson SAS Hotel
Karl-Arnold-Platz 5, Tel. (02 11) 4 55 30, www.radissonsas.com
Rheinhotel Vier Jahreszeiten Meerbusch
Zur Rheinfähre 14/15, Tel. (0 21 50) 91 40, www.rheinhotel-meerbusch.de
Schaper Apartment KG
Hohe Str. 37–41, Tel. (02 11) 86 22 11 00, www.schaper-appartment.com
Swissôtel Düsseldorf/Neuss
Rheinallee 1, Tel. (0 21 31) 77 00, www.swissotel.de

HOTELS * * *

CVJM Hotel Garni
Christlicher Verein junger Menschen Düsseldorf e. V., Graf-Adolf-Str. 102, Tel. (02 11) 17 28 50, www.cvjm-duesseldorf.de
Dorint Hotel Ratingen
An der Pönt 50, Tel. (0 21 02) 91 85
Günnewig Hotel Uebachs
Leopoldstr. 3–5, Tel. (02 11) 17 37 10, www.guennewig.de
Gut Dyckhof-Meerbusch
Am Dyckhof 3, Tel. (0 21 32) 97 77, www.gutdyckhof.de
Haus am Zoo
Sybelstr. 21, Tel. (02 11) 6 16 96 10, www.haus-am-zoo.de
Hotel Astoria
Jahnstr. 72, Tel. (02 11) 38 51 30, www.hotel-astoria-dus.de
Hotel Auszeit
Auf'm Hennekamp 71, Tel. (02 11) 5 13 56 10, www.auszeit-hotel.de
Hotel Batavia
Bahnstr. 61, Tel. (02 11) 36 11 80, www.hotel-batavia.de
Hotel Business Wieland
Wielandstr. 8/corner Am Wehrhahn, Tel. (02 11) 17 30 00, www.Hotel-Wieland.de
Hotel Orangerie
Bäckergasse 1, Tel. (02 11) 86 68 00, www.hotel-orangerie-mcs.de

HOSPITALS

Augusta Krankenhaus
Amalienstr. 9,
Tel. (02 11) 9 04 30

Dominikus-Krankenhaus
Am Heerdter Krankenhaus 2,
Tel. (02 11) 56 70

Evangelisches Krankenhaus
Kirchfeldstr. 40,
Tel. (02 11) 91 90

Florence Nightingale Krankenhaus
Kreuzbergstr. 79,
Tel. (02 11) 40 90

Krankenhaus Benrath
Urdenbacher Allee 83,
Tel. (02 11) 9 97 02

Krankenhaus Elbroich
Am Falder 6,
Tel. (02 11) 7 56 00

Luisen-Krankenhaus
Degerstr. 8,
Tel. (02 11) 69 92 20

Marien Hospital
Rochusstr. 2,
Tel. (02 11) 4 40 00

Marienkrankenhaus Kaiserswerth
An St. Swidbert 17,
Tel. (02 11) 9 40 50

St. Martinus-Krankenhaus
Gladbacher Str. 26,
Tel. (02 11) 91 70

St. Vinzenz-Krankenhaus
Schlossstr. 85,
Tel. (02 11) 9 58 01

Universitätsklinikum Düsseldorf
Moorenstr. 4,
Tel. (02 11) 81 00

DENTAL CLINICS

Zahnklinik dentalästhetica
Kaiserstr. 5,
Tel. (02 11) 49 47 12

Zahnklinik MEDECO
Grafenberger Allee 136,
Tel. (02 11) 6 01 11 11

Hotel Schnellenburg
Rotterdamer Str. 120, Tel. (02 11) 4 38 83, www.schnellenburg.de

InterCityHotel Düsseldorf
Graf-Adolf-Str. 81–87,
Tel. (02 11) 43 69 40,
www.InterCityHotel.com/duesseldorf

Madison Hotel II
Graf-Adolf-Str. 47, Tel. (02 11) 38 80 30

Tulip Inn Düsseldorf Arena
Arena-Str. 3, Tel. (02 11) 30 27 50,
www.tulipinnduesseldorfarena.com

HOTELS * *

Hotel Alt Düsseldorf
Hunsrückenstr. 11,
Tel. (02 11) 13 36 04

Hotel Berial
Gartenstr. 30, Tel. (02 11) 49 00 49-0

Hotel Rosenhof Superior
Bahnhofstr. 2–4, Tel. (02 11) 7 44 11

Ibis Düsseldorf Hauptbahnhof
Konrad-Adenauer-Platz 14,
Tel. (02 11) 1 67 20

Ibis Düsseldorf Zentrum
Ludwig-Erhardt-Allee 2,
Tel. (02 11) 7 70 10

YOUTH HOSTELS

Jugendherberge Düsseldorf
Düsseldorfer Str. 1, Tel. (02 11) 57 70 30, www.djh.de

Kolpinghaus
Blücherstr. 6, Tel. (02 11) 61 70 35 00,
www.kolpinghaeuser.de

INTERNET CAFÉS

E-Commerce-Treff
Berliner Allee 33, Tel. (02 11) 6 00 68 83, www.commerce-treff.de

CoffeNet
Ulmenstr. 11, Tel. (02 11) 4 40 76 07,
www.coffenet.de

Surf Inn
Königsallee 1, Tel. (02 11) (Kaufhof) 1 39 12 13, www.surfinn.com

TICKET OFFICES

RP-Ticket-Shop
Heinrich-Heine-Allee 22, Tel. (02 11) 32 91 91, www.westticket.de

d:Ticket
Immermannstr. 65b, Tel. (0 18 05) 64 43 32, www.dticket.de

TOURIST-INFORMATION

Tourist Information Office at central station
Immermannstraße 65 b
Tel. (0211) 17 20217 202-844
Opening hours Mon. -Fri. 9.30-19.00, Sat. 9.30-17.00

Tourist Information Office Altstadt (Old Town)
Marktstraße/Ecke Rheinstraße
Tel. (0211) 17 202-840
Opening hours Mon. -Sun. 10.00-18.00

CULTURE AND LEISURE

GASTRO AND PARTY